The Apology of Socrates
In Plain and Simple English

BookCaps™ Study Guides
www.bookcaps.com

Cover Image © Stefanos Kyriazis - Fotolia.com

Table of Contents

About This Series

The "Classic Retold" series started as a way of telling classics for the modern reader—being careful to preserve the themes and integrity of the original. Whether you want to understand Shakespeare a little more or are trying to get a better grasps of the Greek classics, there is a book waiting for you!

Modern Version

I do not know, oh Athenians, how much you have been influenced by my accusers; I must say that even I, listening to them, almost forgot my own arguments, as there's worse so plausible. However, they have not actually said anything which was true. But of the many lies they spoke, there was one of them which particularly amazed me, when they said that you ought to be careful not to be deceived by me because I was so eloquent. It seems that they are not ashamed of being shown to be guilty by me, factually, when I show them that I am not in any way eloquent. This seems to me to be the most shameless thing they said, unless by eloquent they mean someone who speaks the truth. If that's what they mean, then I will agree that I am an orator, but I am not the same as them; I repeat, they have said nothing true, and you will hear nothing but the whole truth from me. I'm not going to give you carefully fashioned arguments, as they did, with fine phrases and expressions, and rhetorical flourishes, but you will hear a speech spoken without planning in whatever words first come to hand. I'm confident that what I say will be right, and none of you should expect anything else, for it would not be suitable to my age to appear before you like a young man with a carefully written speech. Athenians, I beg this one thing from you above all else; if you hear me defending myself in the same language as that which I use in the forum and in the shops, where many of you will have heard me speak, and other places, don't be surprised or disturbed by that. For this is the case: this is the first time I have appeared before a court of law, although I am more than seventy years old; so I am completely unfamiliar with the language used here. If I were a foreigner, you would have excuse me speaking in the language and style which reflected my education, so I'm asking you as an act of justice (it seems to me) to ignore the way I speak. Perhaps it may be rather worse, perhaps it may be better, I want you to only think of this, and only pay attention to this; whether what I say is true or not. This is what must be judged, not the skills of an orator.

Firstly, Athenians! What I shall do is to defend myself against the first false allegations made against me, and the first people who accused me, and then I shall defend myself from the latest accusations and the latest accusers. For many years many people have made false accusations against me to you, people of whom I am more afraid than Anytus and his crowd, although they are also formidable adversaries. But even worse are those, Athenians, who have got hold of many of you from childhood and persuaded you to believe things about me which are not true: "There is a wise man called Socrates, who spends his time on heavenly matters, and has explored everything on earth, and makes bad things appear good." Athenians, those who spread around these rumours are my worst accusers, for people who hear them think that those who investigate these matters do not believe that there are gods. The next problem is that there are many of these accusers, and they have now been attacking me for a long time; furthermore, they said these things to you at that point of your life when you were most gullible, when you were boys, some of you young men, and they all accused me in my absence, when there was no one there to defend me. But the most unreasonable thing of all is that it's impossible to discover and broadcast their names, except that I know one of them happens to be a comic poet. However, those who are influenced by envy and lies have persuaded you, and those who allowed themselves to be persuaded have persuaded others, these are the most difficult people to deal with. It isn't possible to bring any of them here, to dismiss their arguments. However, it is very necessary for me to fight as if I were fighting a shadow as I make my defence, and to convince you even know there is no one to answer. So, think, as I have said, that I have two different sorts of accusers, some who have recently accused me, and others long ago, whom I have mentioned. You should agree that I ought to defend myself against the latter sort first, for those are the ones you first heard accusing me, and much more often than the other type.

Well, then I must make my defence, Athenians! I must try in this short space of time to clear your minds of the lies you have heard about me for a long time. I hope that this will happen, being better both for you and for me, and I also wish that in making my defence I could make some even better happen. However, I think that this will be difficult, and I am not completely unaware of what the difficulty is. Nevertheless, let things happen in whatever way is most pleasing to God; I must follow the law and lay out my defence.

So, let us repeat from the start the accusation from which these evil sayings against me have come, which Melitus used as the basis for indicting me. So, what do my accusers say in the charge? It is necessary to read what they have written down as they are public accusers. "Socrates acts wickedly, and is a criminal in the way he investigates things under the earth, and in the heavens, and in the way he makes bad things appear to be good, and teaches the same thing to others." This is the accusation: you have seen things like this in Aristophanes' comedies, with a character called Socrates being carried about, saying that he can walk in the air, and doing many other foolish things which I don't understand at all. I don't say this to put down such a science, if anyone is skilled at such things, but I don't think that Melitus should be prosecuting me for it. I'm saying these things, Athenians, because I have no involvement in such matters at all. I request most of you to be witnesses to this, and to tell each other of it, all of you who have ever heard me speak; there are many of you who have. So if any of you have ever heard me saying a word about such subjects, tell each other. Then you will know that other things of which I'm accused are of a similar nature.

However, not one of these things is true; nor is it true, whatever you may have heard, that I try to teach men and demand payment for it. Even though it seems to me that doing so would be an honourable thing, if one could teach men like Gorgias the Leontine, Prodicus the Cean and Hippias the Elean. For each of these people, O Athenians, go to several cities and persuade the young men, who could attach themselves to any of their own fellow citizens as they wished, to abandon their fellow citizens and go with them, paying them and thanking them as well. There is also another wise man here, a Parian who I have heard is staying in the city. I happened to visit a man who spends more money on teachers of philosophy than anyone else: I mean Callias son of Hipponicus. So I asked him, because he has a pair of sons, " Callias," I said, "if both your sons were colts or calves, we would have had to select a master for them, and to hire a person who can bring out the best in them. He would have been a groom or farmworker. But as your sons have now become men, what master will you choose for them? Who is an expert in how a man and a citizen should behave? I suppose you must have thought about this, since you have sons. Do you know anyone or not?" "Certainly," he answered. "Who is he?" I said, "and where does he come from? What is the charge for his teaching?" He answered, "Evenus the Parian, Socrates, and he charges five minae." I thought that Evenus must be a happy man, if he really does have this skill and teaches it well. I would think very well of myself, and be very proud, if I had this ability, but, Athenians, I do not have it.

Now perhaps somebody might object, "But, Socrates, what have you done? Where have these evil accusations against you come from? Surely if you haven't done more than other people, these rumours and stories would never have been spread around, unless you had acted differently to most men. So tell us what you have done, so that we don't pass hasty judgement on you." Anyone who says that seems to me to be justified, and I will try to show you the reason why I have been suffered these accusations. So listen; some of you might think that I'm joking, but rest assured I will tell you the whole truth. The only thing which has made people think I am like that is that I have a certain wisdom. So what is this wisdom? Perhaps it is just normal human wisdom. In that, truly, I do appear to be wise. Those who I recently mentioned probably have superhuman wisdom, which I can say nothing about, because I am not familiar with it and anyone who says I am is speaking falsely, in order to slander me to. Don't shout out against me, even if you think that I am being rather arrogant. The story I'm going to tell you does not come from me, I shall tell you something which comes from a place which you can believe in. I shall refer you to the god at Delphi as a witness to my wisdom, if I have any, and what sort of wisdom it is. No doubt you know Chaerepho: I knew him when I was young, and most of you did; he went into exile with you, and came home with you. So you know what kind of man Chaerepho was, how seriously he took anything he attempted. Once he went to Delphi, he made this enquiry at the Oracle (and as I said, Athenians, do not shout me down), he asked if there was anyone who was wiser than me. The Oracle answered that no person was wiser; since he is dead, his brother here will confirm what I say.

So, consider why I am saying this: it is because I'm going to demonstrate how these slanders against me began. When I heard this, I thought to myself, "What does the god mean? What mystery is this? I don't think I am wise, not even a little bit. So what does he mean when he says that I'm the wisest? He certainly can't be speaking falsely: that would be impossible. For a long time I was uncertain as to what he meant; afterwards, with great difficulty, I used the following methods to try and discover his meaning. I went to somebody who is reputed to be wise, thinking that meeting him would give me the best chance of proving the Oracle wrong, and demonstrating that this person was wiser than me, even though the Oracle said I was the wisest. So then, having questioned this man (there is no need to mention his name; however, he was one of our great politicians, and in questioning him I felt as I will now tell you, Athenians!), having spoken to him it seemed that he was regarded as wise by most other men, and especially by himself, although in fact he was not. So I tried to show him how he imagined that he was wise, but really was not. In doing this I became hateful, both to him and to many others who were there. When I left him, I thought to myself: I am wiser than this man, because neither of us seems to know anything great or good, but he thinks he does, although he knows nothing. I also know nothing, but I don't imagine anything else. In this little way, then, it seems that I am wiser than him, because I don't imagine that I know something I don't. After that I went to someone who was thought to be wiser than the man I previously met, and I thought that he was much the same. So I became hateful to him and to many other people.

After this I went to visit other men in turn, realising, and being sorry and worried about it, that I was making myself hateful; however it seemed necessary to view the words of the god as being the most important thing, and that to discover the meaning I must visit everyone who had the reputation of being wise. And by God, Athenians, I must tell you the truth, I came to this conclusion: that those who had the greatest reputation seemed to me the most lacking in wisdom and others who were thought of as inferior were closer to having understanding. This is what I found in my researches into what the god said. But I must tell you of my travels, and the work I undertook, in order to prove that the Oracle was correct. After I had spoken to the politicians I went to the poets, the tragic as well as the dithyrambic, expecting to find that I was much more ignorant than them. So I took some of their poems, which seemed to me to be made with great wisdom, and I asked them about their meaning, so that I could learn something from them at the same time. Athenians, I am ashamed to tell you the truth, however it must be told. In a word, almost everybody there could have explained the poems better than those who had written them. I soon discovered, with regard to poets, that they do not achieve their results through wisdom but through natural inspiration and enthusiasm, like prophets and fortune tellers. They also say many fine things, but do not understand what they say. It seems to me that the poets were affected in a similar way, although at the same time I noticed that they thought that because they could write poetry they were the wisest of men in other areas, which they were not. So I left them having been persuaded that I was superior to them, in the same way that I was superior to the politicians.

So at last, I went to the workmen. Whilst I realised that I knew hardly anything, I was sure that I would find they had a great store of useful knowledge. I was not wrong about this, because they knew things I did not and in this way they were wiser than me. But, Athenians, even the best workmen seemed to me to have made the same mistake as the poets. Each one, because he was brilliant at his particular specialty, thought he was very wise in all other important things; this error clouded the wisdom which they truly had. So I asked myself, on behalf of the Oracle, whether it would be better to carry on as I am, having none of either their wisdom or their ignorance, or to have both, like them. I answered, to myself and to the Oracle, that it was better to remain as I am.

So from this investigation, Athenians, I gained many enemies, very terrible and harsh ones, and they committed many slanders against me, including calling me wise; for those who are around from time to time think that I am wise when I show how ignorant others are. However, the god seems to be truly wise, and this is what his oracle means: that human wisdom is hardly worth anything. It is clear that he was not talking about Socrates, he just used my name, as an example, what he meant was, "The wisest man is someone who, like Socrates, knows that he really knows nothing." Still, in obedience to the god, I travel and search and ask about these things, with citizens and foreigners, if I think any of them otherwise. When I see that he is not, I take the side of the god, and show that he is not. Because of this occupation, I have no time to spend much time on the affairs of state or my own affairs; I am in very great poverty because I have been so devoted to serving the god.

As well as this, young men, belonging to the richest families and having plenty of spare time, follow me of their own volition; they take great pleasure in hearing me put men to the test, and they often copy me and try and put others to the test themselves. When they do that, I think, they find many men who think they know something, although they hardly know anything. Those people who are put to the test by then become angry with me, not with them, and say, "Look at that Socrates, he's an awful fellow, he corrupts young men." When anyone asks them how I have corrupted these young men, what I have done or taught them, they can say nothing, for they do not know. However, so that they don't seem foolish, they made the accusations which one could make against any philosophers; "That he investigates things in heaven and under the earth, that he does not believe in gods, and that he makes bad things appear good." I don't think they would be willing to tell the truth, which is that they have been caught out pretending they know things when they know nothing. So, I think, as they are ambitious and passionate and there are many of them, and they have spoken very persuasively about me, for a long time they have filled your ears with slanders against me. Out of these, Melitus, Anytus and Lycon have attacked me. Melitus attacks me on behalf of the poets, Anytus on behalf of the workmen and the politicians, and Lycon on behalf of the rhetoricians. As I said at the start, I would be amazed if I can wash away from your minds a slander which has lasted for so long. This is the truth, Athenians, and I say it without hiding or disguising anything from you, great or small, even though I know that by doing so I am exposing myself to hatred. However, this proves that I am speaking the truth, and that this is the slander against me, and this is what causes it. And if you look into the matter, either now or later, you will find I'm telling the truth.

So, with respect to the charges which my first accusers have aimed at me, let this be a sufficient explanation. Next I will attempt to answer Melitus, that good and patriotic man (as he calls himself) and those who accused me later. Once again, as they are different accusers, let us have a look at their deposition. It is pretty much this: "Socrates behaves criminally in corrupting young men, and in not believing in those gods which the city believes in, but in other strange gods." This is the accusation; let's look at every part of it. It says that I criminally corrupt young men. But I, Athenians, say that Melitus acts criminally, because he makes jokes about serious matters, foolishly placing men on trial whilst pretending to be keen and caring about things which he never took any interest in. This is what I shall try to prove to you.

So, Melitus, tell me, don't you think that is extremely important that young men should be made as good as possible?

Melitus: I do.

Socrates: Well, now, tell the judges who makes them good, you must know as you are so concerned about it, because having discovered that I corrupt them (so you say) you have brought me to trial and accused me. Come on man, tell the judges who makes them better. Are you aware, Melitus, that you are silent and have nothing to say? Don't you think that it's disgraceful, and that it proves what I'm saying, that you never bothered about this? But tell me, friend, who improves them?

Melitus: The laws.

Socrates: I didn't ask that, good sir, I want to know what man, who must know about the laws?

Melitus: These judges here, Socrates.

Socrates: What are you saying, Melitus? Can they teach young men, and make them better?

Melitus: Certainly.

Socrates: Are you talking about all of them, or can some of them do it and others not?

Melitus: All of them.

Socrates: You're speaking well, by Juno! You've found a great crowd of those who could do good. But what else? Can these people here listening make them better, or not?

Melitus: They can, as well.

Socrates: What about the senators?

Melitus: Them too.

Socrates: But, Melitus, do the people who go to the public meetings corrupt the younger men? Or do they all improve them?

Melitus: They do as well.

Socrates: So it seems that all of the Athenians make young men honourable and good apart from me; I'm the only one who corrupts them. Is this what you're saying?

Melitus: That's exactly what I'm saying.

Socrates: You're charging me with something very bad. But tell me, do you think the same applies to horses? Does every man improve them, and there's only one person who spoils them? Or does it happen quite the opposite? Is there only one person who can improve them, or only a very few; I mean the trainers? If every man meddled with and used the horses, wouldn't they spoil them? Doesn't this happen, Melitus, with horses and with all other animals? This certainly is the case, whether or not you and Anytus deny it. Young men would be very lucky if everyone did them good apart from one man who corrupted them. However, Melitus, you have clearly shown that you never showed any interest in young men; and you have given evidence that you are negligent, as you never paid any attention to the area in which you are accusing me.

So explain to us further, Melitus, in the name of Jupiter, whether it's better to live with good or bad citizens? Answer, my friend, I'm not asking you anything difficult. Doesn't the influence of bad people rub off on those who are always near them, and doesn't the good rub off if you are always with good people?

Melitus: Certainly.

Socrates: Is there anyone who would rather be harmed instead of done good by his friends? Answer, my good man, you are legally obliged to. Is there anyone who wishes to have harm done to him?

Melitus: No, surely not.

Socrates: Now then, are you accusing me of corrupting young men, and making them worse, on purpose or by accident?

Melitus: I say, on purpose.

Socrates: So, Melitus, at your time of life you have become so much wiser than me at my age, because you know that evil people always have an evil influence on those closest to them, and good people a good influence. Whereas I have become so ignorant that I don't know that if I make anyone who associates with me depraved, some of his evil will rub off on me; and yet I deliberately make him evil, you say? I can't believe you, Melitus, and I don't think any other man in the world would. Either I don't corrupt young men, or if I do, I don't do it on purpose: so either way you are lying. But if I corrupt them without meaning to, it is not customary to drag somebody to court, you take the person aside and instruct them and admonish them. Clearly if you showed me I was corrupting them, I would stop doing those things I did by accident. But you rejected me, and didn't wish to meet with me or teach me; however you accuse me here, in the place where one usually accuses those who have to be punished, not taught.

So, Athenians, what I have said is now clear, that Melitus never paid the slightest attention to these matters. However, tell us, Melitus, what you say I do to corrupt young men? Aren't you clearly accusing me of teaching them not to believe in the gods of the city, but other strange deities? Aren't you saying that I am corrupting young men by teaching them these things?

Melitus: That's exactly what I'm saying.

Socrates: So, Melitus, by those very gods whom we are now discussing, speak more clearly to me and these people here. I can't understand whether you're saying that some gods exist (in which case then I show that I do believe in gods, and I'm not a total atheist, so can't be accused on that account), but not the ones in which the city believes, other ones. This is what you're accusing me of, that I introduce them to other gods. Or are you saying that I totally don't believe in any gods and that I teach the same thing to others?

Melitus: I say that you don't believe in any gods.

Socrates: This is amazing, Melitus, why do you say this? Don't I believe that the sun and the moon are gods, like the rest of mankind?

Melitus: No, by Jupiter, O judges! He says that the sun is made of stone and that the moon is made of earth.

Socrates: You seem to think that you are accusing
Anaxagoras, my dear Melitus, and so you are
insulting these men with your supposition that they
are so illiterate that they don't know that the books of
Anaxagoras of Clazomene are full of such ideas. The
young men I teach could buy these books down in the
marketplace for a drachma at the most, and then they
could easily mock Socrates if he pretended they were
his own ideas, especially when they are so absurd. So
I ask you, by Jupiter, do you think that I am an
atheist?

Melitus: I do, by Jupiter.

Socrates: What you say is incredible, Melitus, it
seems to me must be unbelievable even to you. It
seems to me, Athenians, that this man is very insolent
and uncontrolled and he has made this accusation
through downright insolence, lack of control and
carelessness. It seems to me that he has set up a
mystery just to make an experiment. Will wise
Socrates know that I am joking, and am contradicting
myself, or will I be able to deceive him and everyone
who listens to me? In my opinion, he clearly
contradicts himself with his accusation, he seems to
be saying that Socrates is guilty of wrongdoing in
being an atheist, and also in believing that there are
gods. Surely this is the behaviour of somebody who is
messing around.

Now, think with me, Athenians, about why it seems to me he is doing so. You, Melitus, you answer me; and the rest of you, as I asked you at the beginning, don't make a fuss if I speak to him in my usual way.

Is there anyone, Melitus, who believes that there are human affairs but that there are no men? Let him answer me, judges, and not make such a fuss. Is there anyone who doesn't believe in horses, but believes that there are things about horses? Who doesn't believe that there are pipers, but believes that there are pipes? There isn't, wonderful man! Since you're not willing to answer, I will answer for you and tell everyone here. But at least answer this: is there anyone who believes that there are things relating to daemons, but who does not believe in daemons?

Melitus: There isn't.

Socrates: How kind of you to have given us your short answer, even though you were forced to by these judges! So you accuse me of believing in and teaching things about daemons, whether they are new or old; so, according to what you have said, I do believe in things about daemons, and you saw this in the indictment. So, if I believe in things about daemons, surely I must also believe that there are daemons. Isn't this the case? It is. I'll assume that you agree, since you have not answered. But when we talk about daemons, aren't we agreed that they are gods, or the children of gods? Do you agree to this or not?

Melitus: Certainly.

Socrates: So, since I admit that there are daemons (which you admit to), if daemons are a type of god, then I say that you are speaking at cross purposes by saying that I don't say that gods exist, and also that I think they do, because I agree that daemons exist. But if daemons are the children of gods, minor ones, nymphs or others, as they are reported to be, how can any man think that the sons of gods can exist but there are no gods? It would be just as foolish for somebody to think that mules exist, the offspring of horses and asses, but not believe in horses and asses. However, Melitus, you have either made this accusation in order to test me, or because he couldn't think of any real crime to accuse me of. Trying to persuade anyone who has the slightest sense that the same person can believe that there are things relating to daemons and to gods, but there are no daemons, gods or heroes, is utterly impossible.

It doesn't seem to me, O Athenians, that I have to put up a long defence against Melitus' accusations; what I have said should be enough. And what I said at the beginning, that there is great public hatred for me, I can assure you it is true. This is what will condemn me, if I am condemned, not Melitus, or Anytus, but the slanders and envy of the crowd, which has already condemned many others–good men–and I think will also condemn others in future. I don't think it will stop with me.

However, perhaps someone will say, "Aren't you ashamed, Socrates, to have followed a course of study which means you now risk death?" I would answer a person who said that, quite correctly, "You are speaking very wrongly, friend, if you think that a man (if he is to be worth anything) should take the risk of life or death into account before doing anything; all he should think of is whether he is acting justly or unjustly, whether he is being a good man or a bad man. According to your reasoning, all those demigods who died at Troy would be awful characters; the son of Thetis would be as bad as the rest; he was so contemptuous of danger, compared to being disgraced, that when his mother, who was a goddess, spoke to him when he was eager to kill Hector, and said something like this, "My son, if you take revenge for the death of your friend Patroclus, and kill Hector, you will die yourself, your death will immediately follow Hector's," he had contempt for death and danger, he was much more afraid of living as a coward having not taken revenge for his friend, and he said, "Can I die immediately when I have punished the guilty one, so that I will not stay here to be ridiculed, next to the curved ships, a useless burden?" Do you think that he cared about death or danger? This is the truth, Athenians: whenever someone has taken up a position, or been placed there by his chief, he should stay there and meet with danger, it seems to me, not caring about death or anything else, as long as he is not disgraced.

So I would be acting strangely if the generals you had chosen to command me told me to go to Potidae, Amphipolis and Delium, and I went there and stayed there like any other person, and risked death; but when God, as I thought and believed, told me that I had to spend my life studying philosophy, and testing myself and others, I should then abandon my post through fear of death or anything else. Then it truly would be justified to bring me to trial, and to accuse me of not believing in the gods, of disobeying the Oracle, fearing death, and thinking I was wise when I was not. To fear death is exactly the same as seeming to be wise when you are not; it involves pretending to know something that you do not know. For all we know death could be the greatest thing ever to come to a man, but men are afraid of it as if they knew perfectly well it was the worst thing. How can this be anything but the most disgraceful ignorance, to imagine that you know something you don't? But perhaps in this matter I am different from most men, and if I were to say that I am wiser in any one area than another, it would be this, that as I don't have any detailed knowledge of what goes on in the underworld, I do not believe that I know it. But to act against the law, and to disobey my superior, whether it is God or a man, I know that that is evil and wrong. So I will never be afraid of or reject things which, for all I know, might be good, in favour of accepting evil which I know is evil. So, even if you send me away now, and don't give in to Anytus, who said that either I shouldn't come here at all, or that if I did I would have to be executed; he told you that if I escaped then all of your sons, studying the teachings of Socrates, would be utterly corrupted; if you now spoke to me in this way, "Socrates, we will not give in to Anytus, but let you go, however only on this condition: that you stop your researches and stop studying philosophy, and if you are found doing so you will be executed." As I said, if you let me go on those terms, I would say this you, "O Athenians! I respect and love you, but I am going to obey God, not you. As long as I am able to, as long as I live, I will not stop studying philosophy. I will not stop warning any of you I come across, saying, as I have always done, 'You great man! As you are an Athenian, from the most powerful and most famous city in the world, renowned for its wisdom and strength, aren't you ashamed of your greed for riches, trying to find how you can get the most, and for glory and honour, but you don't think at all about wisdom or truth, or how to make your soul as perfect as can be?'" If anyone questions what I say, and says that he does care about these things, I won't let him go, I shall question, examine and test him. If it seems to me that he does not have virtue, but pretends that he does, I will criticise him for valuing highly the most worthless things, and not valuing at all those which are most precious. This is how I will treat everyone I meet, young and old, foreign and citizen, but especially you, my fellow citizens, because you are closest to me. For you may rest assured, this is what God wants me to do. And I don't think any better thing has ever happened to you in this city than my wanting to serve God. For all I ever do is try to persuade you, both young and old, not to care about your bodies, your wealth, as much as you do for your soul, and how you can make it most perfect. I tell you that virtue does not come from wealth, but wealth and all other human blessings, public and private, come from virtue. If I am corrupting young men by saying these things, then you can say these things are wrong; but if anyone says that I have said anything else, he is lying. So I must say to you, Athenians, either give into Anytus, or don't, set me free or not, nothing will make me behave differently, even if it meant I would die many times.

Don't mutter amongst yourselves, Athenians, but carry on listening to me, for I think that this thing will do you good. I'm going to tell you some other things, which might make you shout out, but you must not. So, you can rest assured that if you put me to death, being the sort of man I say I am, you won't do me more harm than the harm you do yourselves. Neither Melitus nor Anytus will harm me; they do not have the power, because I do not believe that it is possible for lower men to injure their betters. Perhaps he can have me condemned to death, or exiled, or take away my rights, and he or others might think these were terrible things. However, I do not think they are terrible, I think it is much worse to do what he is now doing, to try and have an innocent man executed. So now, therefore, Athenians, I am not trying to defend myself, as you might think, I'm trying to defend you, in case by condemning me you will cause offence to God and the gifts he has given you. If you excuse me, you will not find it easy to find another like me, although you may think it is ridiculous of me to say so. God sent me to this city in the same way that he might send a little fly to wake up a huge powerful horse, who has become rather lazy due to his size. I am here to wake you up, and to persuade you and criticise you, and to never leave you alone from one day to the next. It will not be easy for you, Athenians, to find another man like me; so, if you take my advice, you will spare me. But perhaps you will be irritable like people woken from their sleep, and strike me, and giving into Anytus will unthinkingly condemn me to death. Then you will spend the rest of your lives asleep, unless God, caring for you, sends you someone else. But I am the person whom God has given to the city. You can see that from this; it is not usual for a man to neglect all his own business, not to look after himself for so many years, and to constantly look after you, talking to each of you separately, like a father or older brother, trying to persuade you to be good. If I had gained any profit from doing this, and been paid for what I did, there would have been some motive for me to behave like this. But now you can see yourselves that those who accuse me, who have slandered me so shamelessly about everything else, have not been so impudent as to charge me with this; they have not brought any witnesses to prove that I either asked for or charged any payment. And I think I can give you enough proof that I'm telling the truth, that is, the fact that I am so poor.

Perhaps you may think it absurd that I, going around, advise you like this in private, and keep myself busy, but that I never appear in the public meetings to give advice to the city. The reason for this is what you have heard me say many times; it is because I am moved by the influence of God, which Melitus has also mentioned in his indictment in order to mock me. This started with me when I was a child, I could hear a sort of voice which, when it is there, stops me from what I was about to do, but does not drive me on. This is what stopped me interfering in public politics, and I think it was quite right. For you can be assured, Athenians, that if I had attempted to meddle with politics, I would have died long ago, and that would have been no good for you or for me. Do not be angry with me for telling you the truth. It is impossible for any man who sincerely opposes either you, or any other crowd, if he stops unfair and illegal things from being done in a city. Anyone who is sincere in his desire for justice, if he wants to keep himself safe for even a short time, should live privately, and not be involved in public affairs.

I will give you strong proof of this, not in words, but in what you value, facts. So hear what has happened to me, so that you can know that I would not give in on any principle of justice through fear of death, even if by not giving in I must die. What I tell you will be annoying and tiresome, but it is true. For, Athenians, I never had any other magisterial office in the city, but I have been a senator. Our tribe of Antioch happened to be ruling the council when you chose to condemn those ten generals who had not saved those who died in the naval battle, which you all decided was against the law. At that time I was the only one on the council who opposed you doing anything against the law, and I voted against you. When the orators were ready to denounce me and to put me in front of the magistrates, and you encouraged them and cheered them, I thought I should face the danger with law and justice on my side. I would not agree to your unfair plans, even though it might mean imprisonment or death. This is what happened when the city was governed by a democracy. But when it became an oligarchy, the Thirty, having ordered me and four others to come to Parliament, told us to bring Leon from his home of Salamis, so he could be executed. They gave similar orders to many others, wanting as many people as possible to be involved in their guilt. At that time I demonstrated, not in words, but in deeds, that I didn't care about dying, if it's not too vulgar to say so, one jot. All I cared about was that I did nothing unjust or unholy. For that government, powerful as it was, did not frighten me enough to make me do something which was not just; when we left the Parliament, the other four went to Salamis, and brought Leon back, but I went home. Maybe I would have been executed for this, if the government hadn't quickly collapsed. There are many witnesses who can tell you about this.

So, do you think that I would have lived so long if I had been involved in public affairs and, acting as a good man should, had helped the cause of justice, and placed this above everything else as I should? Far from it, Athenians! No other man would have done so either. But I, throughout my life, whatever I have done in public or in private, have always been a man who has done nothing in any way contrary to justice, not to anyone, not even those who those who slander me call my disciples. However, I never ruled over anyone, but if anyone wanted to hear me speaking, or to see me following my mission, whether he was young or old, I never refused. Nor do I only speak for money, and stay silent when I am not paid, I allow both rich and poor alike to question me, and, if anyone wants to, they can answer me and hear what I have to say. Whether any of these people turn out to be a good man or not, I cannot fairly be held responsible, because I never promised them any instruction or gave them any teaching. But if anyone says that he has ever learned or heard anything from me in private which other people have not, I can assure you that he is lying.

But why do some people like spending such a long time with me? You have heard why, Athenians! I have told you the whole truth, that they love hearing those who think they are wise but are not being closely questioned, for this is certainly not disagreeable. But I tell you that this duty was given to me by God, by oracles, by dreams, and by every other way in which God orders men to do things. All these things, Athenians, are true, and if they are not they are easy to prove false. For if I am now corrupting some of the young men, and have already corrupted others, surely some of them, having got older, will now have discovered that I gave them bad advice when they were young and would now rise up against me, accuse me and have me punished. Or if they didn't want to do this themselves, some of their family, their fathers, their brothers or other relatives, if their relation ever was damaged by me, would remember it. However, I can see that many of them are here: there is Crito, my contemporary and fellow townsman, father of Critobolus; there is Lysanius of Sphettus, father of Aeschines; there is Antiphon of Cephisus, father of Epigenes. There are those other people as well, whose brothers were just as close to me, namely, Nicostratus, son of Theodotus, brother of Theodotus—Theodotus is dead, so that he could not oppose what his brother is doing—and Paralus here, son of Demodocus, whose brother was Theages; and Adimantus, son of Ariston, whose brother is this Plato; and Æantodorus, whose brother is this Apollodorus. I could also mention many others, at least one of whom Melitus should have mentioned in his speech as a witness. However, if he forgot to do that, let him mention them now; I give him permission to do so, let him say it, if he has any allegation of that kind to make. But, it's rather contrary, you will find, Athenians. Everyone is ready to help me, even though Melitus and Antyus say that I have corrupted and harmed their relatives. Those who have been corrupted themselves might perhaps still help me; but those who have not been corrupted, their relatives, men now of advanced years, what other reason than they have for helping me, except the true and just one which is that they know Melitus is lying and that I am telling the truth?

Well then, Athenians, these are the things which I have to say my defence, along with other things which are similar. Perhaps, however, some of you might object to my being so calm and not producing any children or relatives and friends to beg the judges with tears for mercy, as you may have done in cases of far less importance; I do nothing like this, even though I am in the most extreme danger. So perhaps someone, noticing this, might become angry at my conduct and vote against me. If anyone of you feels like this–I don't suppose anyone does–but if anyone does, I think I can fairly say to him, "Wonderful man, I also have relatives, for to quote Homer, I did not spring up from an oak or a rock but from men, so I also, Athenians, have relatives, I have three sons, one of them is now grown-up and two of them are boys: however, I will not bring any one of them forward to beg you to let me go." So why do I do not do this? It's not from pride, Athenians, nor from disrespect towards you. Whether or not I am scared of death is another question, but to show respect for my own character, and for yours, and for the whole city, I do not think that at my age it would be honourable for me to do anything like this, it would damage the reputation I have, whether it is earned or not. For it is generally agreed that in some ways Socrates is better than other men. So those amongst you who appear to be extremely wise, or strong, or to have any other sort of virtue, were to behave in the fashion which I have seen some do when they have been brought to trial, it would be shameful, when they have pretended to be one thing and then behaved in a different fashion, as if dying would be if something dreadful for them to suffer, and as if they would be immortal if you did not execute them. Men like that seem to me to bring disgrace to the city, so that any foreigner might imagine that those Athenians who have most virtuous and who have been chosen above others to be magistrates and given other honours, are no better than women. Those of us who have gained any sort of reputation should not do these things, Athenians, and if we do, you should not tolerate it. You should make it plain that you would rather condemn anyone who tries these pathetic dramatics, and makes the city looked ridiculous, more than someone who quietly awaits his sentence.

But apart from my reputation, Athenians, it doesn't seem right to me to beg a judge, or to escape through that begging. One should simply tell him the facts and try to persuade him. The judge is not here to give justice to those whom he favours, he is here to judge correctly, and he has sworn that he will not show favour just on his whims, but that he will decide according to the law. Therefore it is right that you should not become accustomed to violating your oaths, and we should not let you, because if we did both of us would be wrong. So do not think, Athenians, that I should behave towards you in a way which I would think would be dishonourable, unjust and impious, by Jupiter, on any other occasion, particularly now when this Melitus is accusing me of being impious. Clearly, if I manage to persuade you, and through my begging managed to turn those of you who are bound by an oath, I would be persuading you to think that there are no gods, and I would be acting as if I did not believe in the gods myself. However, this is far from the case; I do believe in the gods, Athenians, unlike my accusers, and I leave it to you and to God to judge in whatever way is best for me and for you.

[This here Socrates finishes his defence, and once the votes are counted he is declared guilty by a majority. He then carries on speaking.]

But I'm not upset, Athenians, that you have condemned me, along with everything else which has happened. I actually expected this to happen, in fact I'm rather surprised at the balance of the votes. I didn't expect to be condemned by such a small number, I thought there would be a great majority against me; however, it appears that if only three votes had changed sides, I would have been acquitted. I must say that it seems to me as far as Melitus is concerned, I have already been acquitted; not only have I been acquitted, but it's obvious to everyone that if Anytus and Lycon hadn't come forward to accuse me, he would have been fined a thousand drachma for not having been able to raise twenty percent of the vote.

So, this man sentences me to death. Good. But what shall I give myself, Athenians? Isn't it clear that I will give myself what I deserve? So what is that? Do I deserve to suffer, or to pay a fine? Do I deserve this for deliberately not being quiet, but not going after what most men want, wealth, family matters, military commands, popular speechmaking, and all the jobs, conspiracies and factions that one meets the city, thinking that I was really too virtuous to be safe if I became involved in such matters? So I did not follow those pursuits, for by doing so I would have not been able to do any good for you or for me. However, in order to do each of you the greatest good privately, as I have said, I tried to do that, trying to persuade each one of you not to take care of any business before he had taken care of his own soul, and not taking care of the business of the city before he had taken care of the city itself, and to behave in this way in all things. So, seeing as that is what I have done, what treatment do I deserve? If I am judged by my true deserts, Athenians, I would deserve a reward, a reward appropriate to me. So then, what would be a suitable reward for a poor man, a do-gooder, the man who needs time in order to give you good advice? Nothing would be more appropriate than that a man like that should be kept in the city temple, he deserves it much more than somebody who has won a horse race at the Olympic Games, or the two or four horsed chariot race: someone like that makes you think you're happy, but I make you really happy; he does not need supporting, and I do. So if I were to give a sentence according to what I deserve, I would award myself a place in the city temple.

However, perhaps by speaking to you like this you think that I'm speaking in the same arrogant fashion as I did when I was talking about begging judges, but this is not the case. The fact is that I am certain that I have never deliberately harmed any man, although I can't convince you of this, because we have only been speaking to each other for a little while. If the same law applied here as it does in other places, that in cases where execution is the punishment the trial should not just last a single day, but many days, I think you would agree with me, but it is not easy to refute great slanders in just a short time. So, certain that I have harmed nobody, I do not intend to harm myself, and to say that I deserve punishment and give myself anything like that. Through fear of what? In case I suffer through what Melitus gives me, which I have said I do not know if it is good or evil? Instead of this, would I choose what I certainly know is evil, and give myself that? Will I choose imprisonment? Why should I live in prison, as a slave for the established magistrates, the Eleven? Should I choose to be fined, and to be held in prison until it is paid?That'll be the same as what I mentioned before, because I do not have the money to pay. Shall I send myself into exile when? Perhaps you would agree to that. I would really be wanting to hang onto life, Athenians, if I were so foolish that I did not consider the fact that you, my fellow citizens, have found my way of life and speeches so tiresome and horrible that you want to get rid of them–how can I believe that others will put up with them. Far from it, Athenians! A fine life it would be for me at my age to have to wander around, thrown out of city after city, and live my life like that. For I know perfectly well that wherever I go, young men will listen to me when I speak, as they have done here. If they don't like what I say, they will throw me out themselves, persuading the elders to do so. If they do like what I say, their fathers and their families will banish me because of it.

However, perhaps someone will say, Socrates, when you have left us, can you lead a silent and quiet life? This is the most difficult thing to persuade some of you of. I'm telling you that that would mean disobeying God, and so it is therefore impossible for me to live quietly, but if I say this you won't believe me, thinking I'm speaking ironically. On the other hand, if I say that the greatest good a man can do is to speak daily about virtue, and the other things you have heard me discussing, testing both myself and others, and that a life without questioning is not worth living, you would believe me even less. However, I swear to you, Athenians, that this is the case, although you are not easy to persuade. At the same time I don't think that I deserve any punishment. If I were rich, I would find myself a sum which I would be able to pay, for then I would have suffered no harm. However I cannot do that, unless you're willing to find me a sum which I can pay. Perhaps I could pay you a single silver coin: so I fine myself that. But here is Plato, and Crito Critobulus, and Apollodorus, encouraging me to fine myself thirty silver coins, and they offer to stand bail for me. So, I fine myself that amount; they guarantee the money.

[The judges now passed sentence, condemning Socrates to death; so he carried on:]

In order to save a rather short time, Athenians, you have let yourselves in for criticism from those who wish to attack the city, for having executed that wise man, Socrates. Those who want to criticise you will say that I'm wise, although I am not. If you had waited for a short time, this would have happened anyway; see how old I am, you can see that I am close to death. But I'm not saying this to all of you, only those who condemn me to death. And I say this, to the same people. Perhaps you think that I have been convicted because I did not have good enough arguments to persuade you, that if I had just said anything I could escape punishment. This is not the case: I have been convicted not because I did not have arguments, but because I do not have arrogance and impudence, and I will not just say things because you wanted to hear them, I will not lament and wail and do and say things which are unworthy of me, as you usually hear from others. I didn't think that I should, just to avoid danger, do anything unbefitting a freeman of Athens, and I do not regret having defended myself like this. I would much rather die than live having defended myself like that. It is not right in either a trial or battle for me or for anyone else to use any means possible to avoid death. In battle it is frequently obvious that a man could escape death by laying down his arms and surrendering to his enemies. In every dangerous situation there are techniques which would allow a man to avoid death, if he doesn't care what he does and says. Escaping death is not difficult, it is more difficult to avoid lowering oneself, that comes easier than death. And now I, being slow and old, have been caught by slow death, but my accusers, who are strong and active, have been caught by swift wickedness. And now I leave, condemned to death by you, but they are condemned by truth as being guilty of evil and injustice. I will wait for my sentence, and they will too. Perhaps things ought to be like this, and I think they are for the best.

Next, I want to predict what fate has in store for those of you who have condemned me, for I am in the position in which men most frequently prophesy–that is, when they are about to die. So I say to you, Athenians, who have condemned me to death, that as soon as I am dead you will suffer a punishment far more severe, by Jupiter, than the one which you have given me. You have done this, thinking that it would free you from the obligation of having to account for your lives. However, I promise you that exactly the opposite will happen. There will be far more people accusing you, I have kept them back, although you did not know it; and they will be harder on you, because they are younger, and you will object more. If you think that by executing men you can stop people criticising you for not living well, you are very much mistaken. Escaping in this way is neither possible nor honourable; the most honourable and easiest thing to do is not to try and control others, but for each man to consider how he can make himself as perfect as possible. Now that I have predicted this for those of you who condemned me, I shall leave you.

But I would gladly talk about what has happened with those of you who voted for my acquittal whilst the magistrates are busy, and I have not yet been taken off to the place of execution. So stay with me for this little time, Athenians, for there is nothing to stop us talking to each other while we can; I want to let you know, as my friends, the meaning of what has happened to me. A strange thing has happened to me, my judges (I'm giving you your correct name as my judges). The usual voice of prophecy which I have heard from my guardian deity in the past, even in the smallest matters, stopped me if I was about to do anything wrong. But now what you have seen has happened to me, which anyone would think is the worst that could possibly happen, the God did not give me any warning when I left home this morning, nor when I came to this court, nor as I was speaking; but on other occasions it has frequently stopped me in the middle of my speech. But now it never stopped me throughout this trial, in my actions or my words. Why do you think this is? I will tell you: what has happened to me is a blessing, and it is impossible for those who think correctly to imagine that death is an evil thing. I take it as a great proof that unless what is coming to me is good I would have received the usual signal to stop me.

Furthermore, we can conclude from this that there is a great hope that death is a blessing. It can only mean one of two things to die: either the dead are wiped out, and cannot feel anything; or, as people believe, the soul undergoes a change and moves from one place to another. If it is the deprivation of all sensations, as if it were a sleep in which you have no dreams, death would be a wonderful thing. I think that anyone, if he chose a night when he slept so soundly that he did not dream, and compared it with all the other nights and days in his life, and then was asked to say how many days and nights had he spent so pleasurably, I think that not only a private citizen but even the great King himself would find that there were only a small number. So, I say, if death is like this, then it is a gain, for the whole of the future is nothing more than a single night. But if, on the other hand, death is moving from here to another place, and what is believed is true, that all the dead who have gone before are there, what greater blessing is there, my judges? For if, in arriving in the underworld, out of reach of those who pretend they are judges, we find the true judges who are said to judge there, Minos and Rhadamanthus, Aeacus and Triptolemus, and other demigods who were just during their lifetimes, would this be a cause for regret? What would you give to have a meeting with Orpheus and Musaeus, Hesiod and Homer? I would be willing to die many deaths, if this is true. For me it would be wonderful to travel there, where I could meet with Palamedes, and Ajax, son of Telamon, and any other of the ancients who died through an unfair sentence. Comparing my sufferings with theirs would, I think, be rather wonderful. But my greatest pleasure would be to do what I have done on earth, to question and examine the people there and find out who is wise and who thinks he is but is not. What wouldn't you give, my judges, to have the chance of questioning the one who led that mighty army against Troy, or Ulysses, or Sisyphus, or ten thousand others whom one might mention, both men and women; can you imagine what happiness it would be to be able to meet them and speak to them and question them? I'm sure that the judges in the underworld will not sentence you to death for that; in some ways those who live down there are happier than those living on Earth, and once there they are immortal, if what is said is true.

So, my judges, you should look forward to death optimistically, and think about this one truth, that nothing is evil for a good man, neither while he is alive nor when he is dead, and the gods will not forget him. What has happened to me has not happened by chance; but it is clear to me, that it is better for me now to die and be released from my cares. This is why the warning did not come to turn me aside, and I have no resentment towards those who condemned me, or those who accused me, although they did not condemn and accuse me meaning for this to happen, but thinking that they were injuring me: they deserve to be criticised for that.

However, I beg this favour from them. When my sons grow up, punish them, give them the same pain I have given you, if they seem to care about riches or anything else before goodness; if they think that they are something when they are nothing, criticise them as I have criticised you, for not paying attention to what they should, and for thinking that they are something when they are worth nothing. If you do this for me, my sons and I will both have had good treatment from you.

But now it is time to go–I am going to die, you're going to live. But only God knows which of us is going to a better place.

Comparative Version

I know not, O Athenians! how far you have been influenced by my accusers; for my part, in listening to them I almost forgot myself, so plausible were their arguments however, so to speak, they have said nothing true. But of the many falsehoods which they uttered I wondered at one of them especially, that in which they said that you ought to be on your guard lest you should be deceived by me, as being eloquent in speech. For that they are not ashamed of being forthwith convicted by me in fact, when I shall show that I am not by any means eloquent, this seemed to me the most shameless thing in them, unless indeed they call him eloquent who speaks the truth. For, if they mean this, then I would allow that I am an orator, but not after their fashion for they, as I affirm, have said nothing true, but from me you shall hear the whole truth. Not indeed, Athenians, arguments highly wrought, as theirs were, with choice phrases and expressions, nor adorned, but you shall hear a speech uttered without premeditation in such words as first present themselves. For I am confident that what I say will be just, and let none of you expect otherwise, for surely it would not become my time of life to come before you like a youth with a got up speech. Above all things, therefore, I beg and implore this of you, O Athenians! if you hear me defending myself in the same language as that in which I am accustomed to speak both in the forum at the counters, where many of you have heard me, and elsewhere, not to be surprised or disturbed on this account. For the case is this: I now for the first time come before a court of justice, though more than seventy years old; I am therefore utterly a stranger to the language here. As, then, if I were really a stranger, you would have pardoned me if I spoke in the language and the manner in which I had been educated, so now I ask this of you as an act of justice, as it appears to me, to disregard the manner of my speech, for perhaps it may be somewhat worse, and perhaps better, and to consider this only, and to give your attention to this, whether I speak what is just or not; for this is the virtue of a judge, but of an orator to speak the truth.

I do not know, oh Athenians, how much you have been influenced by my accusers; I must say that even I, listening to them, almost forgot my own arguments, as there's worse so plausible. However, they have not actually said anything which was true. But of the many lies they spoke, there was one of them which particularly amazed me, when they said that you ought to be careful not to be deceived by me because I was so eloquent. It seems that they are not ashamed of being shown to be guilty by me, factually, when I show them that I am not in any way eloquent. This seems to me to be the most shameless thing they said, unless by eloquent they mean someone who speaks the truth. If that's what they mean, then I will agree that I am an orator, but I am not the same as them; I repeat, they have said nothing true, and you will hear nothing but the whole truth from me. I'm not going to give you carefully fashioned arguments, as they did, with fine phrases and expressions, and rhetorical flourishes, but you will hear a speech spoken without planning in whatever words first come to hand. I'm confident that what I say will be right, and none of you should expect anything else, for it would not be suitable to my age to appear before you like a young man with a carefully written speech. Athenians, I beg this one thing from you above all else; if you hear me defending myself in the same language as that which I use in the forum and in the shops, where many of you will have heard me speak, and other places, don't be surprised or disturbed by that. For this is the case: this is the first time I have appeared before a court of law, although I am more than seventy years old; so I am completely unfamiliar with the language used here. If I were a foreigner, you would have excuse me speaking in the language and style which reflected my education, so I'm asking you as an act of justice (it seems to me) to ignore the way I speak. Perhaps it may be rather worse, perhaps it may be better, I want you to only think of this, and only pay attention to this; whether what I say is true or not. This is what must be judged, not the skills of an orator.

2. First, then, O Athenians! I am right in defending myself against the first false accusations alleged against me, and my first accusers, and then against the latest accusations, and the latest accusers. For many have been accusers of me to you, and for many years, who have asserted nothing true, of whom I am more afraid than of Anytus and his party, although they too are formidable; but those are still more formidable, Athenians, who, laying hold of many of you from childhood, have persuaded you, and accused me of what is not true: "that there is one Socrates, a wise man, who occupies himself about celestial matters, and has explored every thing under the earth, and makes the worse appear the better reason." Those, O Athenians! who have spread abroad this report are my formidable accusers; for they who hear them think that such as search into these things do not believe that there are gods. In the next place, these accusers are numerous, and have accused me now for a long time; moreover, they said these things to you at that time of life in which you were most credulous, when you were boys and some of you youths, and they accused me altogether in my absence, when there was no one to defend me. But the most unreasonable thing of all is, that it is not possible to learn and mention their names, except that one of them happens to be a comic poet.1 Such, however, as, influenced by envy and calumny, have persuaded you, and those who, being themselves persuaded, have persuaded others, all these are most difficult to deal with; for it is not possible to bring any of them forward here, nor to confute any; but it is altogether necessary to fight, as it were with a

shadow, in making my defense, and to convict when there is no one to answer. Consider, therefore, as I have said, that my accusers are twofold, some who have lately accused me, and others long since, whom I have made mention of; and believe that I ought to defend myself against these first; for you heard them accusing me first, and much more than these last.

Firstly, Athenians! What I shall do is to defend myself against the first false allegations made against me, and the first people who accused me, and then I shall defend myself from the latest accusations and the latest accusers. For many years many people have made false accusations against me to you, people of whom I am more afraid than Anytus and his crowd, although they are also formidable adversaries. But even worse are those, Athenians, who have got hold of many of you from childhood and persuaded you to believe things about me which are not true: "There is a wise man called Socrates, who spends his time on heavenly matters, and has explored everything on earth, and makes bad things appear good." Athenians, those who spread around these rumours are my worst accusers, for people who hear them think that those who investigate these matters do not believe that there are gods. The next problem is that there are many of these accusers, and they have now been attacking me for a long time; furthermore, they said these things to you at that point of your life when you were most gullible, when you were boys, some of you young men, and they all accused me in my absence, when there was no one there to defend me. But the most unreasonable thing of all is that it's impossible to discover and broadcast their names, except that I know one of them happens to be a comic poet. However, those who are influenced by envy and lies have persuaded you, and those who allowed themselves to be persuaded have persuaded others, these are the most difficult people to deal with. It isn't possible to bring any of them here, to dismiss their arguments. However, it is very necessary for me to

fight as if I were fighting a shadow as I make my
defence, and to convince you even know there is no
one to answer. So, think, as I have said, that I have
two different sorts of accusers, some who have
recently accused me, and others long ago, whom I
have mentioned. You should agree that I ought to
defend myself against the latter sort first, for those
are the ones you first heard accusing me, and much
more often than the other type.

Well. I must make my defense, then, O Athenians!
and endeavor in this so short a space of time to
remove from your minds the calumny which you have
long entertained. I wish, indeed, it might be so, if it
were at all better both for you and me, and that in
making my defense I could effect something more
advantageous still: I think, however, that it will be
difficult, and I am not entirely ignorant what the
difficulty is. Nevertheless, let this turn out as may be
pleasing to God, I must obey the law and make my
defense.

Well, then I must make my defence, Athenians! I must
try in this short space of time to clear your minds of
the lies you have heard about me for a long time. I
hope that this will happen, being better both for you
and for me, and I also wish that in making my defence
I could make some even better happen. However, I
think that this will be difficult, and I am not
completely unaware of what the difficulty is.
Nevertheless, let things happen in whatever way is
most pleasing to God; I must follow the law and lay
out my defence.

---

3. Let us, then, repeat from the beginning what the accusation is from which the calumny against me has arisen, and relying on which Melitus has preferred this indictment against me. Well. What, then, do they who charge me say in their charge? For it is necessary to read their deposition as of public accusers. "Socrates acts wickedly, and is criminally curious in searching into things under the earth, and in the heavens, and in making the worse appear the better cause, and in teaching these same things to others." Such is the accusation: for such things you have yourselves seen in the comedy of Aristophanes, one Socrates there carried about, saying that he walks in the air, and acting many other buffooneries, of which I understand nothing whatever. Nor do I say this as disparaging such a science, if there be any one skilled in such things, only let me not be prosecuted by Melitus on a charge of this kind; but I say it, O Athenians! because I have nothing to do with such matters. And I call upon most of you as witnesses of this, and require you to inform and tell each other, as many of you as have ever heard me conversing; and there are many such among you. Therefore tell each other, if any one of you has ever heard me conversing little or much on such subjects. And from this you will know that other things also, which the multitude assert of me, are of a similar nature.

So, let us repeat from the start the accusation from which these evil sayings against me have come, which Melitus used as the basis for indicting me. So, what do my accusers say in the charge? It is necessary to read what they have written down as they are public accusers. "Socrates acts wickedly, and is a criminal in the way he investigates things under the earth, and in the heavens, and in the way he makes bad things appear to be good, and teaches the same thing to others." This is the accusation: you have seen things like this in Aristophanes' comedies, with a character called Socrates being carried about, saying that he can walk in the air, and doing many other foolish things which I don't understand at all. I don't say this to put down such a science, if anyone is skilled at such things, but I don't think that Melitus should be prosecuting me for it. I'm saying these things, Athenians, because I have no involvement in such matters at all. I request most of you to be witnesses to this, and to tell each other of it, all of you who have ever heard me speak; there are many of you who have. So if any of you have ever heard me saying a word about such subjects, tell each other. Then you will know that other things of which I'm accused are of a similar nature.

4. However not one of these things is true; nor, if you have heard from any one that I attempt to teach men, and require payment, is this true. Though this, indeed, appears to me to be an honorable thing, if one should be able to instruct men, like Gorgias the Leontine, Prodicus the Cean, and Hippias the Elean. For each of these, O Athenians! is able, by going through the several cities, to persuade the young men, who can attach themselves gratuitously to such of their own fellow-citizens as they please, to abandon their fellow-citizens and associate with them, giving them money and thanks besides. There is also another wise man here, a Parian, who, I hear, is staying in the city. For I happened to visit a person who spends more money on the sophists than all others together: I mean Callias, son of Hipponicus. I therefore asked him, for he has two sons, "Callias," I said, "if your two sons were colts or calves, we should have had to choose a master for them, and hire a person who would make them excel in such qualities as belong to their nature; and he would have been a groom or an agricultural laborer. But now, since your sons are men, what master do you intend to choose for them? Who is there skilled in the qualities that become a man and a citizen? For I suppose you must have considered this, since you have sons. Is there any one," I said, "or not?" "Certainly," he answered. "Who is he?" said I, "and whence does he come? and on what terms does he teach?" He replied, "Evenus the Parian, Socrates, for five minæ." And I deemed Evenus happy, if he really possesses this art, and teaches admirably. And I too should think highly of myself, and be very proud, if I possessed this knowledge, but I possess it not, O

Athenians.

However, not one of these things is true; nor is it true, whatever you may have heard, that I try to teach men and demand payment for it. Even though it seems to me that doing so would be an honourable thing, if one could teach men like Gorgias the Leontine, Prodicus the Cean and Hippias the Elean. For each of these people, O Athenians, go to several cities and persuade the young men, who could attach themselves to any of their own fellow citizens as they wished, to abandon their fellow citizens and go with them, paying them and thanking them as well. There is also another wise man here, a Parian who I have heard is staying in the city. I happened to visit a man who spends more money on teachers of philosophy than anyone else: I mean Callias son of Hipponicus. So I asked him, because he has a pair of sons, "Callias," I said, "if both your sons were colts or calves, we would have had to select a master for them, and to hire a person who can bring out the best in them. He would have been a groom or farmworker. But as your sons have now become men, what master will you choose for them? Who is an expert in how a man and a citizen should behave? I suppose you must have thought about this, since you have sons. Do you know anyone or not?" "Certainly," he answered. "Who is he?" I said, "and where does he come from? What is the charge for his teaching?" He answered, "Evenus the Parian, Socrates, and he charges five minae." I thought that Evenus must be a happy man, if he really does have this skill and teaches it well. I would think very well of myself, and be very proud, if I had this ability, but, Athenians, I do not have it.

5. Perhaps, one of you may now object: "But, Socrates, what have you done, then? Whence have these calumnies against you arisen? For surely if you had not busied yourself more than others, such a report and story would never have got abroad, unless you had done something different from what most men do. Tell us, therefore, what it is, that we may not pass a hasty judgment on you." He who speaks thus appears to me to speak justly, and I will endeavor to show you what it is that has occasioned me this character and imputation. Listen, then: to some of you perhaps I shall appear to jest, yet be assured that I shall tell you the whole truth. For I, O Athenians! have acquired this character through nothing else than a certain wisdom. Of what kind, then, is this wisdom? Perhaps it is merely human wisdom. For in this, in truth, I appear to be wise. They probably, whom I have just now mentioned, possessed a wisdom more than human, otherwise I know not what to say about it; for I am not acquainted with it, and whosoever says I am, speaks falsely, and for the purpose of calumniating me. But, O Athenians! do not cry out against me, even though I should seem to you to speak somewhat arrogantly. For the account which I am going to give you is not my own; but I shall refer to an authority whom you will deem worthy of credit. For I shall adduce to you the god at Delphi as a witness of my wisdom, if I have any, and of what it is. You doubtless know Chærepho: he was my associate from youth, and the associate of most of you; he accompanied you in your late exile, and returned with you. You know, then, what kind of a man Chærepho was, how earnest in whatever he

undertook. Having once gone to Delphi, he ventured to make the following inquiry of the oracle (and, as I said, O Athenians! do not cry out), for he asked if there was any one wiser than I. The Pythian thereupon answered that there was not one wiser; and of this, his brother here will give you proofs, since he himself is dead.

Now perhaps somebody might object, "But, Socrates, what have you done? Where have these evil accusations against you come from? Surely if you haven't done more than other people, these rumours and stories would never have been spread around, unless you had acted differently to most men. So tell us what you have done, so that we don't pass hasty judgement on you." Anyone who says that seems to me to be justified, and I will try to show you the reason why I have been suffered these accusations. So listen; some of you might think that I'm joking, but rest assured I will tell you the whole truth. The only thing which has made people think I am like that is that I have a certain wisdom. So what is this wisdom? Perhaps it is just normal human wisdom. In that, truly, I do appear to be wise. Those who I recently mentioned probably have superhuman wisdom, which I can say nothing about, because I am not familiar with it and anyone who says I am is speaking falsely, in order to slander me to. Don't shout out against me, even if you think that I am being rather arrogant. The story I'm going to tell you does not come from me, I shall tell you something which comes from a place which you can believe in. I shall refer you to the god at Delphi as a witness to my wisdom, if I have any, and what sort of wisdom it is. No doubt you know Chaerepho: I knew him when I was young, and most of you did; he went into exile with you, and came home with you. So you know what kind of man Chaerepho was, how seriously he took anything he attempted. Once he went to Delphi, he made this enquiry at the Oracle (and as I said, Athenians, do not shout me down), he asked if there was anyone who was wiser than me. The Oracle answered that no person was wiser; since he is dead, his brother here will confirm what I say.

6. Consider, then, why I mention these things: it is because I am going to show you whence the calumny against me arose. For when I heard this, I reasoned thus with myself, What does the god mean? What enigma is this? For I am not conscious to myself that I am wise, either much or little. What, then, does he mean by saying that I am the wisest? For assuredly he does not speak falsely: that he could not do. And for a long time I was in doubt what he meant; afterward, with considerable difficulty, I had recourse to the following method of searching out his meaning. I went to one of those who have the character of being wise, thinking that there, if anywhere, I should confute the oracle, and show in answer to the response that This man is wiser than I, though you affirmed that I was the wisest. Having, then, examined this man (for there is no occasion to mention his name; he was, however, one of our great politicians, in examining whom I felt as I proceed to describe, O Athenians!), having fallen into conversation with him, this man appeared to be wise in the opinion of most other men, and especially in his own opinion, though in fact he was not so. I thereupon endeavored to show him that he fancied himself to be wise, but really was not. Hence I became odious, both to him and to many others who were present. When I left him, I reasoned thus with myself: I am wiser than this man, for neither of us appears to know anything great and good; but he fancies he knows something, although he knows nothing; whereas I, as I do not know anything, so I do not fancy I do. In this trifling particular, then, I appear to be wiser than he, because I do not fancy I know

what I do not know. After that I went to another who was thought to be wiser than the former, and formed the very same opinion. Hence I became odious to him and to many others.

So, consider why I am saying this: it is because I'm going to demonstrate how these slanders against me began. When I heard this, I thought to myself, "What does the god mean? What mystery is this? I don't think I am wise, not even a little bit. So what does he mean when he says that I'm the wisest? He certainly can't be speaking falsely: that would be impossible. For a long time I was uncertain as to what he meant; afterwards, with great difficulty, I used the following methods to try and discover his meaning. I went to somebody who is reputed to be wise, thinking that meeting him would give me the best chance of proving the Oracle wrong, and demonstrating that this person was wiser than me, even though the Oracle said I was the wisest. So then, having questioned this man (there is no need to mention his name; however, he was one of our great politicians, and in questioning him I felt as I will now tell you, Athenians!), having spoken to him it seemed that he was regarded as wise by most other men, and especially by himself, although in fact he was not. So I tried to show him how he imagined that he was wise, but really was not. In doing this I became hateful, both to him and to many others who were there. When I left him, I thought to myself: I am wiser than this man, because neither of us seems to know anything great or good, but he thinks he does, although he knows nothing. I also know nothing, but I don't imagine anything else. In this little way, then, it seems that I am wiser than him, because I don't imagine that I know something I don't. After that I went to someone who was thought to be wiser than the man I previously met, and I thought that he was

much the same. So I became hateful to him and to
many other people.

7. After this I went to others in turn, perceiving indeed, and grieving and alarmed, that I was making myself odious; however, it appeared necessary to regard the oracle of the god as of the greatest moment, and that, in order to discover its meaning, I must go to all who had the reputation of possessing any knowledge. And by the dog, O Athenians! for I must tell you the truth, I came to some such conclusion as this: those who bore the highest reputation appeared to me to be most deficient, in my researches in obedience to the god, and others who were considered inferior more nearly approaching to the possession of understanding. But I must relate to you my wandering, and the labors which I underwent, in order that the oracle might prove incontrovertible. For after the politicians I went to the poets, as well the tragic as the dithyrambic and others, expecting that here I should in very fact find myself more ignorant than they. Taking up, therefore, some of their poems, which appeared to me most elaborately finished, I questioned them as to their meaning, that at the same time I might learn something from them. I am ashamed, O Athenians! to tell you the truth; however, it must be told. For, in a word, almost all who were present could have given a better account of them than those by whom they had been composed. I soon discovered this, therefore, with regard to the poets, that they do not effect their object by wisdom, but by a certain natural inspiration, and under the influence of enthusiasm, like prophets and seers; for these also say many fine things, but they understand nothing that they say. The poets appeared to me to be affected in a similar manner; and at the

same time I perceived that they considered
themselves, on account of their poetry, to be the
wisest of men in other things, in which they were not.
I left them, therefore, under the persuasion that I was
superior to them, in the same way that I was to the
politicians.

After this I went to visit other men in turn, realising, and being sorry and worried about it, that I was making myself hateful; however it seemed necessary to view the words of the god as being the most important thing, and that to discover the meaning I must visit everyone who had the reputation of being wise. And by God, Athenians, I must tell you the truth, I came to this conclusion: that those who had the greatest reputation seemed to me the most lacking in wisdom and others who were thought of as inferior were closer to having understanding. This is what I found in my researches into what the god said. But I must tell you of my travels, and the work I undertook, in order to prove that the Oracle was correct. After I had spoken to the politicians I went to the poets, the tragic as well as the dithyrambic, expecting to find that I was much more ignorant than them. So I took some of their poems, which seemed to me to be made with great wisdom, and I asked them about their meaning, so that I could learn something from them at the same time. Athenians, I am ashamed to tell you the truth, however it must be told. In a word, almost everybody there could have explained the poems better than those who had written them. I soon discovered, with regard to poets, that they do not achieve their results through wisdom but through natural inspiration and enthusiasm, like prophets and fortune tellers. They also say many fine things, but do not understand what they say. It seems to me that the poets were affected in a similar way, although at the same time I noticed that they thought that because they could write poetry they were the wisest of men in other areas, which they were not. So I left them

*having been persuaded that I was superior to them, in
the same way that I was superior to the politicians.*

8. At last, therefore, I went to the artisans. For I was
conscious to myself that I knew scarcely anything,
but I was sure that I should find them possessed of
much beautiful knowledge. And in this I was not
deceived; for they knew things which I did not, and in
this respect they were wiser than I. But, O Athenians!
even the best workmen appeared to me to have fallen
into the same error as the poets; for each, because he
excelled in the practice of his art, thought that he was
very wise in other most important matters, and this
mistake of theirs obscured the wisdom that they really
possessed. I therefore asked myself, in behalf of the
oracle, whether I should prefer to continue as I am,
possessing none, either of their wisdom or their
ignorance, or to have both as they have. I answered,
therefore, to myself and to the oracle, that it was
better for me to continue as I am.

So at last, I went to the workmen. Whilst I realised that I knew hardly anything, I was sure that I would find they had a great store of useful knowledge. I was not wrong about this, because they knew things I did not and in this way they were wiser than me. But, Athenians, even the best workmen seemed to me to have made the same mistake as the poets. Each one, because he was brilliant at his particular specialty, thought he was very wise in all other important things; this error clouded the wisdom which they truly had. So I asked myself, on behalf of the Oracle, whether it would be better to carry on as I am, having none of either their wisdom or their ignorance, or to have both, like them. I answered, to myself and to the Oracle, that it was better to remain as I am.

9. From this investigation, then, O Athenians! many enmities have arisen against me, and those the most grievous and severe, so that many calumnies have sprung from them, and among them this appellation of being wise; for those who are from time to time present think that I am wise in those things, with respect to which I expose the ignorance of others. The god, however, O Athenians! appears to be really wise, and to mean this by his oracle: that human wisdom is worth little or nothing; and it is clear that he did not say this to Socrates, but made use of my name, putting me forward as an example, as if he had said, that man is the wisest among you, who, like Socrates, knows that he is in reality worth nothing with respect to wisdom. Still, therefore, I go about and search and inquire into these things, in obedience to the god, both among citizens and strangers, if I think any one of them is wise; and when he appears to me not to be so, I take the part of the god, and show that he is not wise. And, in consequence of this occupation, I have no leisure to attend in any considerable degree to the affairs of the state or my own; but I am in the greatest poverty through my devotion to the service of the god.

So from this investigation, Athenians, I gained many enemies, very terrible and harsh ones, and they committed many slanders against me, including calling me wise; for those who are around from time to time think that I am wise when I show how ignorant others are. However, the god seems to be truly wise, and this is what his oracle means: that human wisdom is hardly worth anything. It is clear that he was not talking about Socrates, he just used my name, as an example, what he meant was, "The wisest man is someone who, like Socrates, knows that he really knows nothing." Still, in obedience to the god, I travel and search and ask about these things, with citizens and foreigners, if I think any of them otherwise. When I see that he is not, I take the side of the god, and show that he is not. Because of this occupation, I have no time to spend much time on the affairs of state or my own affairs; I am in very great poverty because I have been so devoted to serving the god.

10. In addition to this, young men, who have much leisure and belong to the wealthiest families, following me of their own accord, take great delight in hearing men put to the test, and often imitate me, and themselves attempt to put others to the test; and then, I think, they find a great abundance of men who fancy they know something, although they know little or nothing. Hence those who are put to the test by them are angry with me, and not with them, and say that "there is one Socrates, a most pestilent fellow, who corrupts the youth." And when any one asks them by doing or teaching what, they have nothing to say, for they do not know; but, that they may not seem to be at a loss, they say such things as are ready at hand against all philosophers; "that he searches into things in heaven and things under the earth, that he does not believe there are gods, and that he makes the worse appear the better reason." For they would not, I think, be willing to tell the truth that they have been detected in pretending to possess knowledge, whereas they know nothing. Therefore, I think, being ambitions and vehement and numerous, and speaking systematically and persuasively about me, they have filled your ears, for a long time and diligently calumniating me. From among these, Melitus, Anytus and Lycon have attacked me; Melitus being angry on account of the poets, Anytus on account of the artisans and politicians, and Lycon on account of the rhetoricians. So that, as I said in the beginning, I should wonder if I were able in so short a time to remove from your minds a calumny that has prevailed so long. This, O Athenians! is the truth; and I speak it without concealing or disguising anything from you,

much or little; though I very well know that by so doing I shall expose myself to odium. This, however, is a proof that I speak the truth, and that this is the nature of the calumny against me, and that these are its causes. And if you will investigate the matter, either now or hereafter, you will find it to be so.

As well as this, young men, belonging to the richest families and having plenty of spare time, follow me of their own volition; they take great pleasure in hearing me put men to the test, and they often copy me and try and put others to the test themselves. When they do that, I think, they find many men who think they know something, although they hardly know anything. Those people who are put to the test by then become angry with me, not with them, and say, "Look at that Socrates, he's an awful fellow, he corrupts young men." When anyone asks them how I have corrupted these young men, what I have done or taught them, they can say nothing, for they do not know. However, so that they don't seem foolish, they made the accusations which one could make against any philosophers; "That he investigates things in heaven and under the earth, that he does not believe in gods, and that he makes bad things appear good." I don't think they would be willing to tell the truth, which is that they have been caught out pretending they know things when they know nothing. So, I think, as they are ambitious and passionate and there are many of them, and they have spoken very persuasively about me, for a long time they have filled your ears with slanders against me. Out of these, Melitus, Anytus and Lycon have attacked me. Melitus attacks me on behalf of the poets, Anytus on behalf of the workmen and the politicians, and Lycon on behalf of the rhetoricians. As I said at the start, I would be amazed if I can wash away from your minds a slander which has lasted for so long. This is the truth, Athenians, and I say it without hiding or disguising anything from you, great or small, even though I know that by

doing so I am exposing myself to hatred. However,
this proves that I am speaking the truth, and that this
is the slander against me, and this is what causes it.
And if you look into the matter, either now or later,
you will find I'm telling the truth.

11. With respect, then, to the charges which my first
accusers have alleged against me, let this be a
sufficient apology to you. To Melitus, that good and
patriotic man, as he says, and to my later accusers, I
will next endeavor to give an answer; and here, again,
as there are different accusers, let us take up their
deposition. It is pretty much as follows: "Socrates," it
says, "acts unjustly in corrupting the youth, and in not
believing in those gods in whom the city believes, but
in other strange divinities." Such is the accusation; let
us examine each particular of it. It says that I act
unjustly in corrupting the youth. But I, O Athenians!
say that Melitus acts unjustly, because he jests on
serious subjects, rashly putting men upon trial, under
pretense of being zealous and solicitous about things
in which he never at any time took any concern. But
that this is the case I will endeavor to prove to you.

So, with respect to the charges which my first accusers have aimed at me, let this be a sufficient explanation. Next I will attempt to answer Melitus, that good and patriotic man (as he calls himself) and those who accused me later. Once again, as they are different accusers, let us have a look at their deposition. It is pretty much this: "Socrates behaves criminally in corrupting young men, and in not believing in those gods which the city believes in, but in other strange gods." This is the accusation; let's look at every part of it. It says that I criminally corrupt young men. But I, Athenians, say that Melitus acts criminally, because he makes jokes about serious matters, foolishly placing men on trial whilst pretending to be keen and caring about things which he never took any interest in. This is what I shall try to prove to you.

12. Come, then, Melitus, tell me, do you not consider it of the greatest importance that the youth should be made as virtuous as possible?

Mel. I do.

Socr. Well, now, tell the judges who it is that makes them better, for it is evident that you know, since it concerns you so much; for, having detected me in corrupting them, as you say, you have cited me here, and accused me: come, then, say, and inform the judges who it is that makes them better. Do you see, Melitus, that you are silent, and have nothing to say? But does it not appear to you to be disgraceful, and a sufficient proof of what I say, that you never took any concern about the matter? But tell me, friend, who makes them better?

Mel. The laws.

Socr. I do not ask this, most excellent sir, but what man, who surely must first know this very thing, the laws?

Mel. These, Socrates, the judges.

Socr. How say you, Melitus? Are these able to instruct the youth, and make them better?

Mel. Certainly.

Socr. Whether all, or some of them, and others not?

Mel. All.

Socr. You say well, by Juno! and have found a great abundance of those that confer benefit. But what further? Can these hearers make them better, or not?

Mel. They, too, can.

Socr. And what of the senators?

Mel. The senators, also.

Socr. But, Melitus, do those who attend the public assemblies corrupt the younger men? or do they all make them better?

Mel. They too.

Socr. All the Athenians, therefore, as it seems, make them honorable and good, except me; but I alone corrupt them. Do you say so?

Mel. I do assert this very thing.

Socr. You charge me with great ill-fortune. But answer me: does it appear to you to be the same, with respect to horses? Do all men make them better, and is there only some one that spoils them? or does quite the contrary of this take place? Is there some one person who can make them better, or very few; that is, the trainers? But if the generality of men should meddle with and make use of horses, do they spoil them? Is not this the case, Melitus, both with respect to horses and all other animals? It certainly is so, whether you and Anytus deny it or not. For it would be a great good-fortune for the youth if only one person corrupted, and the rest benefited them. However, Melitus, you have sufficiently shown that you never bestowed any care upon youth; and you clearly evince your own negligence, in that you have never paid any attention to the things with respect to which you accuse me.

So, Melitus, tell me, don't you think that is extremely important that young men should be made as good as possible?

Melitus: I do.

Socrates: Well, now, tell the judges who makes them good, you must know as you are so concerned about it, because having discovered that I corrupt them (so you say) you have brought me to trial and accused me. Come on man, tell the judges who makes them better. Are you aware, Melitus, that you are silent and have nothing to say? Don't you think that it's disgraceful, and that it proves what I'm saying, that you never bothered about this? But tell me, friend, who improves them?

Melitus: The laws.

Socrates: I didn't ask that, good sir, I want to know what man, who must know about the laws?

Melitus: These judges here, Socrates.

Socrates: What are you saying, Melitus? Can they teach young men, and make them better?

Melitus: Certainly.

Socrates: Are you talking about all of them, or can some of them do it and others not?

Melitus: All of them.

Socrates: You're speaking well, by Juno! You've found a great crowd of those who could do good. But what else? Can these people here listening make them better, or not?

Melitus: They can, as well.

Socrates: What about the senators?

Melitus: Them too.

Socrates: But, Melitus, do the people who go to the public meetings corrupt the younger men? Or do they all improve them?

Melitus: They do as well.

Socrates: So it seems that all of the Athenians make young men honourable and good apart from me; I'm the only one who corrupts them. Is this what you're saying?

Melitus: That's exactly what I'm saying.

Socrates: You're charging me with something very bad. But tell me, do you think the same applies to horses? Does every man improve them, and there's only one person who spoils them? Or does it happen quite the opposite? Is there only one person who can improve them, or only a very few; I mean the trainers? If every man meddled with and used the horses, wouldn't they spoil them? Doesn't this happen, Melitus, with horses and with all other animals? This certainly is the case, whether or not you and Anytus deny it. Young men would be very lucky if everyone did them good apart from one man who corrupted them. However, Melitus, you have clearly shown that you never showed any interest in young men; and you have given evidence that you are negligent, as you never paid any attention to the area in which you are accusing me.

13. Tell us further, Melitus, in the name of Jupiter, whether is it better to dwell with good or bad citizens? Answer, my friend; for I ask you nothing difficult. Do not the bad work some evil to those that are continually near them, but the good some good?

Mel. Certainly.

Socr. Is there any one that wishes to be injured rather than benefited by his associates? Answer, good man; for the law requires you to answer. Is there any one who wishes to be injured?

Mel. No, surely.

Socr. Come, then, whether do you accuse me here, as one that corrupts the youth, and makes them more depraved, designedly or undesignedly?

Mel. Designedly, I say.

Socr. What, then, Melitus, are you at your time of life so much wiser than I at my time of life, as to know that the evil are always working some evil to those that are most near to them, and the good some good; but I have arrived at such a pitch of ignorance as not to know that if I make any one of my associates depraved, I shall be in danger of receiving some evil from him; and yet I designedly bring about this so great evil, as you say? In this I can not believe you, Melitus, nor do I think would any other man in the world. But either I do not corrupt the youth, or, if I do corrupt them, I do it undesignedly: so that in both cases you speak falsely. But if I corrupt them undesignedly, for such involuntary offenses it is not usual to accuse one here, but to take one apart, and teach and admonish one. For it is evident that if I am taught, I shall cease doing what I do undesignedly. But you shunned me, and were not willing to associate with and instruct me; but you accuse me here, where it is usual to accuse those who need punishment, and not instruction.

So explain to us further, Melitus, in the name of Jupiter, whether it's better to live with good or bad citizens? Answer, my friend, I'm not asking you anything difficult. Doesn't the influence of bad people rub off on those who are always near them, and doesn't the good rub off if you are always with good people?

Melitus: Certainly.

Socrates: Is there anyone who would rather be harmed instead of done good by his friends? Answer, my good man, you are legally obliged to. Is there anyone who wishes to have harm done to him?

Melitus: No, surely not.

Socrates: Now then, are you accusing me of corrupting young men, and making them worse, on purpose or by accident?

Melitus: I say, on purpose.

Socrates: So, Melitus, at your time of life you have become so much wiser than me at my age, because you know that evil people always have an evil influence on those closest to them, and good people a good influence. Whereas I have become so ignorant that I don't know that if I make anyone who associates with me depraved, some of his evil will rub off on me; and yet I deliberately make him evil, you say? I can't believe you, Melitus, and I don't think any other man in the world would. Either I don't corrupt young men, or if I do, I don't do it on purpose: so either way you are lying. But if I corrupt them without meaning to, it is not customary to drag somebody to court, you take the person aside and instruct them and admonish them. Clearly if you showed me I was corrupting them, I would stop doing those things I did by accident. But you rejected me, and didn't wish to meet with me or teach me; however you accuse me here, in the place where one usually accuses those who have to be punished, not taught.

14. Thus, then, O Athenians! this now is clear that I have said; that Melitus never paid any attention to these matters, much or little. However, tell us, Melitus, how you say I corrupt the youth? Is it not evidently, according to the indictment which you have preferred, by teaching them not to believe in the gods in whom the city believes, but in other strange deities? Do you not say that, by teaching these things, I corrupt the youth?

Mel. Certainly I do say so.

Socr. By those very gods, therefore, Melitus, of whom the discussion now is, speak still more clearly both to me and to these men. For I can not understand whether you say that I teach them to believe that there are certain gods (and in that case I do believe that there are gods, and am not altogether an atheist, nor in this respect to blame), not, however, those which the city believes in, but others; and this it is that you accuse me of, that I introduce others. Or do you say outright that I do not myself believe that there are gods, and that I teach others the same?

Mel. I say this: that you do not believe in any gods at all.

Socr. O wonderful Melitus, how come you to say this? Do I not, then, like the rest of mankind, believe that the sun and moon are gods?

Mel. No, by Jupiter, O judges! for he says that the sun is a stone, and the moon an earth.

Socr. You fancy that you are accusing Anaxagoras, my dear Melitus, and thus you put a slight on these men, and suppose them to be so illiterate as not to know that the books of Anaxagoras of Clazomene are full of such assertions. And the young, moreover, learn these things from me, which they might purchase for a drachma, at most, in the orchestra, and so ridicule Socrates, if he pretended they were his own, especially since they are so absurd? I ask then, by Jupiter, do I appear to you to believe that there is no god?

Mel. No, by Jupiter, none whatever.

Socr. You say what is incredible, Melitus, and that, as appears to me, even to yourself. For this man, O Athenians! appears to me to be very insolent and intemperate and to have preferred this indictment through downright insolence, intemperance, and wantonness. For he seems, as it were, to have composed an enigma for the purpose of making an experiment. Whether will Socrates the wise know that I am jesting, and contradict myself, or shall I deceive him and all who hear me? For, in my opinion, he clearly contradicts himself in the indictment, as if he should say, Socrates is guilty of wrong in not believing that there are gods, and in believing that there are gods. And this, surely, is the act of one who is trifling.

So, Athenians, what I have said is now clear, that Melitus never paid the slightest attention to these matters. However, tell us, Melitus, what you say I do to corrupt young men? Aren't you clearly accusing me of teaching them not to believe in the gods of the city, but other strange deities? Aren't you saying that I am corrupting young men by teaching them these things?

Melitus: That's exactly what I'm saying.

Socrates: So, Melitus, by those very gods whom we are now discussing, speak more clearly to me and these people here. I can't understand whether you're saying that some gods exist (in which case then I show that I do believe in gods, and I'm not a total atheist, so can't be accused on that account), but not the ones in which the city believes, other ones. This is what you're accusing me of, that I introduce them to other gods. Or are you saying that I totally don't believe in any gods and that I teach the same thing to others?

Melitus: I say that you don't believe in any gods.

Socrates: This is amazing, Melitus, why do you say this? Don't I believe that the sun and the moon are gods, like the rest of mankind?

Melitus: No, by Jupiter, O judges! He says that the sun is made of stone and that the moon is made of earth.

Socrates: You seem to think that you are accusing Anaxagoras, my dear Melitus, and so you are insulting these men with your supposition that they are so illiterate that they don't know that the books of Anaxagoras of Clazomene are full of such ideas. The young men I teach could buy these books down in the marketplace for a drachma at the most, and then they could easily mock Socrates if he pretended they were his own ideas, especially when they are so absurd. So I ask you, by Jupiter, do you think that I am an atheist?

Melitus: I do, by Jupiter.

Socrates: What you say is incredible, Melitus, it seems to me must be unbelievable even to you. It seems to me, Athenians, that this man is very insolent and uncontrolled and he has made this accusation through downright insolence, lack of control and carelessness. It seems to me that he has set up a mystery just to make an experiment. Will wise Socrates know that I am joking, and am contradicting myself, or will I be able to deceive him and everyone who listens to me? In my opinion, he clearly contradicts himself with his accusation, he seems to be saying that Socrates is guilty of wrongdoing in being an atheist, and also in believing that there are gods. Surely this is the behaviour of somebody who is messing around.

15. Consider with me now, Athenians, in what respect he appears to me to say so. And do you, Melitus, answer me; and do ye, as I besought you at the outset, remember not to make an uproar if I speak after my usual manner.

Is there any man, Melitus, who believes that there are human affairs, but does not believe that there are men? Let him answer, judges, and not make so much noise. Is there any one who does not believe that there are horses, but that there are things pertaining to horses? or who does not believe that there are pipers, but that there are things pertaining to pipes? There is not, O best of men! for since you are not willing to answer, I say it to you and to all here present. But answer to this at least: is there any one who believes that there are things relating to demons, but does not believe that there are demons?

Mel. There is not.

Socr. How obliging you are in having hardly answered; though compelled by these judges! You assert, then, that I do believe and teach things relating to demons, whether they be new or old; therefore, according to your admission, I do believe in things relating to demons, and this you have sworn in the bill of indictment. If, then, I believe in things relating to demons, there is surely an absolute necessity that I should believe that there are demons. Is it not so? It is. For I suppose you to assent, since you do not answer. But with respect to demons, do we not allow that they are gods, or the children of gods? Do you admit this or not?

Mel. Certainly.

Socr. Since, then, I allow that there are demons, as you admit, if demons are a kind of gods, this is the point in which I say you speak enigmatically and divert yourself in saying that I do not allow there are gods, and again that I do allow there are, since I allow that there are demons? But if demons are the children of gods, spurious ones, either from nymphs or any others, of whom they are reported to be, what man can think that there are sons of gods, and yet that there are not gods? For it would be just as absurd as if any one should think that there are mules, the offspring of horses and asses, but should not think there are horses and asses. However, Melitus, it can not be otherwise than that you have preferred this indictment for the purpose of trying me, or because you were at a loss what real crime to allege against me; for that you should persuade any man who has the smallest degree of sense that the same person can think that there are things relating to demons and to gods, and yet that there are neither demons, nor gods, not heroes, is utterly impossible.

Now, think with me, Athenians, about why it seems to me he is doing so. You, Melitus, you answer me; and the rest of you, as I asked you at the beginning, don't make a fuss if I speak to him in my usual way.

Is there anyone, Melitus, who believes that there are human affairs but that there are no men? Let him answer me, judges, and not make such a fuss. Is there anyone who doesn't believe in horses, but believes that there are things about horses? Who doesn't believe that there are pipers, but believes that there are pipes? There isn't, wonderful man! Since you're not willing to answer, I will answer for you and tell everyone here. But at least answer this: is there anyone who believes that there are things relating to daemons, but who does not believe in daemons?

Melitus: There isn't.

Socrates: How kind of you to have given us your short answer, even though you were forced to by these judges! So you accuse me of believing in and teaching things about daemons, whether they are new or old; so, according to what you have said, I do believe in things about daemons, and you saw this in the indictment. So, if I believe in things about daemons, surely I must also believe that there are daemons. Isn't this the case? It is. I'll assume that you agree, since you have not answered. But when we talk about daemons, aren't we agreed that they are gods, or the children of gods? Do you agree to this or not?

Melitus: Certainly.

Socrates: So, since I admit that there are daemons (which you admit to), if daemons are a type of god, then I say that you are speaking at cross purposes by saying that I don't say that gods exist, and also that I think they do, because I agree that daemons exist. But if daemons are the children of gods, minor ones, nymphs or others, as they are reported to be, how can any man think that the sons of gods can exist but there are no gods? It would be just as foolish for somebody to think that mules exist, the offspring of horses and asses, but not believe in horses and asses. However, Melitus, you have either made this accusation in order to test me, or because he couldn't think of any real crime to accuse me of. Trying to persuade anyone who has the slightest sense that the same person can believe that there are things relating to daemons and to gods, but there are no daemons, gods or heroes, is utterly impossible.

16. That I am not guilty, then, O Athenians! according to the indictment of Melitus, appears to me not to require a lengthened defense; but what I have said is sufficient. And as to what I said at the beginning, that there is a great enmity toward me among the multitude, be assured it is true. And this it is which will condemn me, if I am condemned, not Melitus, nor Anytus, but the calumny and envy of the multitude, which have already condemned many others, and those good men, and will, I think, condemn others also; for there is no danger that it will stop with me.

Perhaps, however, some one may say, "Are you not ashamed, Socrates, to have pursued a study from which you are now in danger of dying?" To such a person I should answer with good reason, You do not say well, friend, if you think that a man, who is even of the least value, ought to take into the account the risk of life or death, and ought not to consider that alone when be performs any action, whether he is acting justly or unjustly, and the part of a good man or bad man. For, according to your reasoning, all those demi-gods that died at Troy would be vile characters, as well all the rest as the son of Thetis, who so far despised danger in comparison of submitting to disgrace, that when his mother, who was a goddess, spoke to him, in his impatience to kill Hector, something to this effect, as I think,"My son, if you revenge the death of your friend Patroclus, and slay Hector, you will yourself die, for," she said, "death awaits you immediately after Hector;" but he, on hearing this, despised death and danger, and dreading much more to live as a coward, and not avenge his friend, said, "May I die immediately when I have inflicted punishment on the guilty, that I may not stay here an object of ridicule, by the curved ships, a burden to the ground?"—do you think that he cared for death and danger? For thus it is, O Athenians! in truth: wherever any one has posted himself, either thinking it to be better, or has been posted by his chief, there, as it appears to me, he ought to remain and meet danger, taking no account either of death or anything else in comparison with disgrace.

It doesn't seem to me, O Athenians, that I have to put up a long defence against Melitus' accusations; what I have said should be enough. And what I said at the beginning, that there is great public hatred for me, I can assure you it is true. This is what will condemn me, if I am condemned, not Melitus, or Anytus, but the slanders and envy of the crowd, which has already condemned many others–good men–and I think will also condemn others in future. I don't think it will stop with me.

However, perhaps someone will say, "Aren't you ashamed, Socrates, to have followed a course of study which means you now risk death?" I would answer a person who said that, quite correctly, "You are speaking very wrongly, friend, if you think that a man (if he is to be worth anything) should take the risk of life or death into account before doing anything; all he should think of is whether he is acting justly or unjustly, whether he is being a good man or a bad man. According to your reasoning, all those demigods who died at Troy would be awful characters; the son of Thetis would be as bad as the rest; he was so contemptuous of danger, compared to being disgraced, that when his mother, who was a goddess, spoke to him when he was eager to kill Hector, and said something like this, "My son, if you take revenge for the death of your friend Patroclus, and kill Hector, you will die yourself, your death will immediately follow Hector's," he had contempt for death and danger, he was much more afraid of living as a coward having not taken revenge for his friend, and he said, "Can I die immediately when I have punished the guilty one, so that I will not stay here to be ridiculed, next to the curved ships, a useless burden?" Do you think that he cared about death or danger? This is the truth, Athenians: whenever someone has taken up a position, or been placed there by his chief, he should stay there and meet with danger, it seems to me, not caring about death or anything else, as long as he is not disgraced.

17. I then should be acting strangely, O Athenians! if, when the generals whom you chose to command me assigned me my post at Potidæa, at Amphipolis, and at Delium, I then remained where they posted me, like any other person, and encountered the danger of death; but when the deity, as I thought and believed, assigned it as my duty to pass my life in the study of philosophy, and examining myself and others, I should on that occasion, through fear of death or any thing else whatsoever, desert my post, strange indeed would it be; and then, in truth, any one might justly bring me to trial, and accuse me of not believing in the gods, from disobeying the oracle, fearing death, and thinking myself to be wise when I am not. For to fear death, O Athenians! is nothing else than to appear to be wise, without being so; for it is to appear to know what one does not know. For no one knows but that death is the greatest of all good to man; but men fear it, as if they well knew that it is the greatest of evils. And how is not this the most reprehensible ignorance, to think that one knows what one does not know? But I, O Athenians! in this, perhaps, differ from most men; and if I should say that I am in any thing wiser than another, it would be in this, that not having a competent knowledge of the things in Hades, I also think that I have not such knowledge. But to act unjustly, and to disobey my superior, whether God or man, I know is evil and base. I shall never, therefore, fear or shun things which, for aught I know, maybe good, before evils which I know to be evils. So that, even if you should now dismiss me, not yielding to the instances of Anytus, who said that either I should not3 appear here at all, or that, if I did

appear, it was impossible not to put me to death, telling you that if I escaped, your sons, studying what Socrates teaches, would all be utterly corrupted; if you should address me thus, "Socrates, we shall not now yield to Anytus, but dismiss you, on this condition, however, that you no longer persevere in your researches nor study philosophy; and if hereafter you are detected in so doing, you shall die"—if, as I said, you should dismiss, me on these terms, I should say to you, "O Athenians! I honor and love you; but I shall obey God rather than you; and so long as I breathe and am able, I shall not cease studying philosophy, and exhorting you and warning any one of you I may happen to meet, saying, as I have been accustomed to do: 'O best of men! seeing you are an Athenian, of a city the most powerful and most renowned for wisdom and strength, are you not ashamed of being careful for riches, how you may acquire them in greatest abundance, and for glory, and honor, but care not nor take any thought for wisdom and truth, and for your soul, how it maybe made most perfect?'" And if any one of you should question my assertion, and affirm that he does care for these things, I shall not at once let him go, nor depart, but I shall question him, sift and prove him. And if he should appear to me not to possess virtue, but to pretend that he does, I shall reproach him for that he sets the least value on things of the greatest worth, but the highest on things that are worthless. Thus I shall act to all whom I meet, both young and old, stranger and citizen, but rather to you, my fellow-citizens, because ye are more nearly allied to me. For be well assured, this the deity commands. And I think that no greater good has ever befallen you in the city than my zeal for the service of the god. For I go about doing nothing else than persuading you, both young and old, to take no care either for the body, or for riches, prior to or so much as for the soul, how it may be made most perfect, telling you that virtue does not spring from riches, but riches and all other human blessings, both private and public, from virtue. If, then, by saying these things, I corrupt the youth, these things must be mischievous; but if any one says that I speak other things than these, he misleads you.4 Therefore I must say, O Athenians! either yield to Anytus, or do not, either dismiss me or not, since I shall not act otherwise, even though I must die many deaths.

So I would be acting strangely if the generals you had chosen to command me told me to go to Potidae, Amphipolis and Delium, and I went there and stayed there like any other person, and risked death; but when God, as I thought and believed, told me that I had to spend my life studying philosophy, and testing myself and others, I should then abandon my post through fear of death or anything else. Then it truly would be justified to bring me to trial, and to accuse me of not believing in the gods, of disobeying the Oracle, fearing death, and thinking I was wise when I was not. To fear death is exactly the same as seeming to be wise when you are not; it involves pretending to know something that you do not know. For all we know death could be the greatest thing ever to come to a man, but men are afraid of it as if they knew perfectly well it was the worst thing. How can this be anything but the most disgraceful ignorance, to imagine that you know something you don't? But perhaps in this matter I am different from most men, and if I were to say that I am wiser in any one area than another, it would be this, that as I don't have any detailed knowledge of what goes on in the underworld, I do not believe that I know it. But to act against the law, and to disobey my superior, whether it is God or a man, I know that that is evil and wrong. So I will never be afraid of or reject things which, for all I know, might be good, in favour of accepting evil which I know is evil. So, even if you send me away now, and don't give in to Anytus, who said that either I shouldn't come here at all, or that if I did I would have to be executed; he told you that if I escaped then all of your sons, studying the teachings of Socrates, would be utterly corrupted; if you now spoke to me in this way, "Socrates, we will not give in to Anytus, but let you go, however only on this condition: that you stop your researches and stop studying philosophy, and if you are found doing so you will be executed." As I said, if you let me go on those terms, I would say this you, "O Athenians! I respect and love you, but I am going to obey God, not you. As long as I am able to, as long as I live, I will not stop studying philosophy. I will not stop warning any of you I come across, saying, as I have always done, 'You great man! As you are an Athenian, from the most powerful and most famous city in the world, renowned for its wisdom and strength, aren't you ashamed of your greed for riches, trying to find how you can get the most, and for glory and honour, but you don't think at all about wisdom or truth, or how to make your soul as perfect as can be?'" If anyone questions what I say, and says that he does care about these things, I won't let him go, I shall question, examine and test him. If it seems to me that he does not have virtue, but pretends that he does, I will criticise him for valuing highly the most worthless things, and not valuing at all those which are most precious. This is how I will treat everyone I meet, young and old, foreign and citizen, but especially you, my fellow citizens, because you are closest to me. For you may rest assured, this is what God wants me to do. And I don't think any better thing has ever happened to you in this city than my wanting to serve God. For all I ever do is try to persuade you, both young and old, not to care about your bodies, your wealth, as much as you do for your soul, and how you can make it most perfect. I tell you that virtue does not come from wealth, but wealth and all other human blessings, public and private, come from virtue. If I am corrupting young men by saying these things, then you can say these things are wrong; but if anyone says that I have said anything else, he is lying. So I must say to you, Athenians, either give into Anytus, or don't, set me free or not, nothing will make me behave differently, even if it meant I would die many times.

18. Murmur not, O Athenians! but continue to attend to my request, not to murmur at what I say, but to listen, for, as I think, you will derive benefit from listening. For I am going to say other things to you, at which, perhaps, you will raise a clamor; but on no account do so. Be well assured, then, if you put me to death, being such a man as I say I am, you will not injure me more than yourselves. For neither will Melitus nor Anytus harm me; nor have they the power; for I do not think that it is possible for a better man to be injured by a worse. He may perhaps have me condemned to death, or banished, or deprived of civil rights; and he or others may perhaps consider these as mighty evils; I, how ever, do not consider them so, but that it is much more so to do what he is now doing, to endeavor to put a man to death unjustly. Now, therefore, O Athenians! I am far from making a defense on my behalf, as any one might think, but I do so on your own behalf, lest by condemning me you should offend at all with respect to the gift of the deity to you. For, if you should put me to death, you will not easily find such another, though it may be ridiculous to say so, altogether attached by the deity to this city as to a powerful and generous horse, somewhat sluggish from his size, and requiring to be roused by a gad-fly; so the deity appears to have united me, being such a person as I am, to the city, that I may rouse you, and persuade and reprove every one of you, nor ever cease besetting you throughout the whole day. Such another man, O Athenians! will not easily be found; therefore, if you will take my advice, you will spare me. But you, perhaps, being irritated like drowsy persons who

are roused from sleep, will strike me, and, yielding to Anytus, will unthinkingly condemn me to death; and then you will pass the rest of your life in sleep, unless the deity, caring for you, should send some one else to you. But that I am a person who has been given by the deity to this city, you may discern from hence; for it is not like the ordinary conduct of men, that I should have neglected all my own affairs, and suffered my private interest to be neglected for so many years, and that I should constantly attend to your concerns, addressing myself to each of you separately, like a father, or elder brother, persuading you to the pursuit of virtue. And if I had derived any profit from this course, and had received pay for my exhortations, there would have been some reason for my conduct; but now you see yourselves that my accusers, who have so shamelessly calumniated me in everything else, have not had the impudence to charge me with this, and to bring witnesses to prove that I ever either exacted or demanded any reward. And I think I produce a sufficient proof that I speak the truth, namely, my poverty.

Don't mutter amongst yourselves, Athenians, but carry on listening to me, for I think that this thing will do you good. I'm going to tell you some other things, which might make you shout out, but you must not. So, you can rest assured that if you put me to death, being the sort of man I say I am, you won't do me more harm than the harm you do yourselves. Neither Melitus nor Anytus will harm me; they do not have the power, because I do not believe that it is possible for lower men to injure their betters. Perhaps he can have me condemned to death, or exiled, or take away my rights, and he or others might think these were terrible things. However, I do not think they are terrible, I think it is much worse to do what he is now doing, to try and have an innocent man executed. So now, therefore, Athenians, I am not trying to defend myself, as you might think, I'm trying to defend you, in case by condemning me you will cause offence to God and the gifts he has given you. If you excuse me, you will not find it easy to find another like me, although you may think it is ridiculous of me to say so. God sent me to this city in the same way that he might send a little fly to wake up a huge powerful horse, who has become rather lazy due to his size. I am here to wake you up, and to persuade you and criticise you, and to never leave you alone from one day to the next. It will not be easy for you, Athenians, to find another man like me; so, if you take my advice, you will spare me. But perhaps you will be irritable like people woken from their sleep, and strike me, and giving into Anytus will unthinkingly condemn me to death. Then you will spend the rest of your lives asleep, unless God, caring for you, sends you someone else. But I am the person whom God has given to the city. You can see that from this; it is not usual for a man to neglect all his own business, not to look after himself for so many years, and to constantly look after you, talking to each of you separately, like a father or older brother, trying to persuade you to be good. If I had gained any profit from doing this, and been paid for what I did, there would have been some motive for me to behave like this. But now you can see yourselves that those who accuse me, who have slandered me so shamelessly about everything else, have not been so impudent as to charge me with this; they have not brought any witnesses to prove that I either asked for or charged any payment. And I think I can give you enough proof that I'm telling the truth, that is, the fact that I am so poor.

19. Perhaps, however, it may appear absurd that I, going about, thus advise you in private and make myself busy, but never venture to present myself in public before your assemblies and give advice to the city. The cause of this is that which you have often and in many places heard me mention; because I am moved by a certain divine and spiritual influence, which also Melitus, through mockery, has set out in the indictment. This began with me from childhood, being a kind of voice which, when present, always diverts me from what I am about to do, but never urges me on. This it is which opposed my meddling in public politics; and it appears to me to have opposed me very properly. For be well assured, O Athenians! if I had long since attempted to intermeddle with politics, I should have perished long ago, and should not have at all benefited you or myself. And be not angry with me for speaking the truth. For it is not possible that any man should be safe who sincerely opposes either you, or any other multitude, and who prevents many unjust and illegal actions from being committed in a city; but it is necessary that he who in earnest contends for justice, if he will be safe for but a short time, should live privately, and take no part in public affairs.

Perhaps you may think it absurd that I, going around, advise you like this in private, and keep myself busy, but that I never appear in the public meetings to give advice to the city. The reason for this is what you have heard me say many times; it is because I am moved by the influence of God, which Melitus has also mentioned in his indictment in order to mock me. This started with me when I was a child, I could hear a sort of voice which, when it is there, stops me from what I was about to do, but does not drive me on. This is what stopped me interfering in public politics, and I think it was quite right. For you can be assured, Athenians, that if I had attempted to meddle with politics, I would have died long ago, and that would have been no good for you or for me. Do not be angry with me for telling you the truth. It is impossible for any man who sincerely opposes either you, or any other crowd, if he stops unfair and illegal things from being done in a city. Anyone who is sincere in his desire for justice, if he wants to keep himself safe for even a short time, should live privately, and not be involved in public affairs.

20. I will give you strong proofs of this, not words, but what you value, facts. Hear, then, what has happened to me, that you may know that I would not yield to any one contrary to what is just, through fear of death, at the same time by not yielding I must perish. I shall tell you what will be displeasing and wearisome,5 yet true. For I, O Athenians! never bore any other magisterial office in the city, but have been a senator: and our Antiochean tribe happened to supply the Prytanes when you chose to condemn in a body the ten generals who had not taken off those that perished in the sea-fight, in violation of the law, as you afterward all thought. At that time I alone of the Prytanes opposed your doing anything contrary to the laws, and I voted against you; and when the orators were ready to denounce me, and to carry me before a magistrate, and you urged and cheered them on, I thought I ought rather to meet the danger with law and justice on my side, than through fear of imprisonment or death, to take part with you in your unjust designs. And this happened while the city was governed by a democracy. But when it became an oligarchy, the Thirty, having sent for me with four others to the Tholus, ordered us to bring Leon the Salaminian from Salamis, that he might be put to death; and they gave many similar orders to many others, wishing to involve as many as they could in guilt. Then, however, I showed, not in word but in deed, that I did not care for death, if the expression be not too rude, in the smallest degree; but that all my care was to do nothing unjust or unholy. For that government, strong as it was, did not so overawe me as to make me commit an unjust action; but when we

came out from the Tholus, the four went to Salamis, and brought back Leon; but I went away home. And perhaps for this I should have been put to death, if that government had not been speedily broken up. And of this you can have many witnesses.

I will give you strong proof of this, not in words, but in what you value, facts. So hear what has happened to me, so that you can know that I would not give in on any principle of justice through fear of death, even if by not giving in I must die. What I tell you will be annoying and tiresome, but it is true. For, Athenians, I never had any other magisterial office in the city, but I have been a senator. Our tribe of Antioch happened to be ruling the council when you chose to condemn those ten generals who had not saved those who died in the naval battle, which you all decided was against the law. At that time I was the only one on the council who opposed you doing anything against the law, and I voted against you. When the orators were ready to denounce me and to put me in front of the magistrates, and you encouraged them and cheered them, I thought I should face the danger with law and justice on my side. I would not agree to your unfair plans, even though it might mean imprisonment or death. This is what happened when the city was governed by a democracy. But when it became an oligarchy, the Thirty, having ordered me and four others to come to Parliament, told us to bring Leon from his home of Salamis, so he could be executed. They gave similar orders to many others, wanting as many people as possible to be involved in their guilt. At that time I demonstrated, not in words, but in deeds, that I didn't care about dying, if it's not too vulgar to say so, one jot. All I cared about was that I did nothing unjust or unholy. For that government, powerful as it was, did not frighten me enough to make me do something which was not just; when we left the Parliament, the other four went to

Salamis, and brought Leon back, but I went home. Maybe I would have been executed for this, if the government hadn't quickly collapsed. There are many witnesses who can tell you about this.

21. Do you think, then, that I should have survived so many years if I had engaged in public affairs, and, acting as becomes a good man, had aided the cause of justice, and, as I ought, had deemed this of the highest importance? Far from it, O Athenians! nor would any other man have done so. But I, through the whole of my life, if I have done anything in public, shall be found to be a man, and the very same in private, who has never made a concession to any one contrary to justice, neither to any other, nor to any one of these whom my calumniators say are my disciples. I, however, was never the preceptor of any one; but if any one desired to hear me speaking, and to see me busied about my own mission, whether he were young or old, I never refused him. Nor do I discourse when I receive money, and not when I do not receive any, but I allow both rich and poor alike to question me, and, if any one wishes it, to answer me and hear what I have to say. And for these, whether any one proves to be a good man or not, I cannot justly be responsible, because I never either promised them any instruction or taught them at all. But if any one says that he has ever learned or heard anything from me in private which all others have not, be well assured that he does not speak the truth.

So, do you think that I would have lived so long if I had been involved in public affairs and, acting as a good man should, had helped the cause of justice, and placed this above everything else as I should? Far from it, Athenians! No other man would have done so either. But I, throughout my life, whatever I have done in public or in private, have always been a man who has done nothing in any way contrary to justice, not to anyone, not even those who those who slander me call my disciples. However, I never ruled over anyone, but if anyone wanted to hear me speaking, or to see me following my mission, whether he was young or old, I never refused. Nor do I only speak for money, and stay silent when I am not paid, I allow both rich and poor alike to question me, and, if anyone wants to, they can answer me and hear what I have to say. Whether any of these people turn out to be a good man or not, I cannot fairly be held responsible, because I never promised them any instruction or gave them any teaching. But if anyone says that he has ever learned or heard anything from me in private which other people have not, I can assure you that he is lying.

22. But why do some delight to spend so long a time with me? Ye have heard, O Athenians! I have told you the whole truth, that they delight to hear those closely questioned who think that they are wise but are not; for this is by no means disagreeable. But this duty, as I say, has been enjoined me by the deity, by oracles, by dreams, and by every mode by which any other divine decree has ever enjoined anything to man to do. These things, O Athenians! are both true, and easily confuted if not true. For if I am now corrupting some of the youths, and have already corrupted others, it were fitting, surely, that if any of them, having become advanced in life, had discovered that I gave them bad advice when they were young, they should now rise up against me, accuse me, and have me punished; or if they were themselves unwilling to do this, some of their kindred, their fathers, or brothers, or other relatives, if their kinsman have ever sustained any damage from me, should now call it to mind. Many of them, however, are here present, whom I see: first, Crito, my contemporary and fellow-burgher, father of this Critobulus; then Lysanias of Sphettus, father of this Æschines; again, Antiphon of Cephisus, father of Epigenes. There are those others, too, whose brothers maintained the same intimacy with me, namely, Nicostratus, son of Theodotus, brother of Theodotus—Theodotus indeed is dead, so that he could not deprecate his brother's proceedings—and Paralus here, son of Demodocus, whose brother was Theages; and Adimantus, son of Ariston, whose brother is this Plato; and Æantodorus, whose brother is this Apollodorus. I could also mention many others to you, some one of whom

certainly Melitus ought to have adduced in his speech as a witness. If, however, he then forgot to do so, let him now adduce them; I give him leave to do so, and let him say it, if he has anything of the kind to allege. But, quite contrary to this, you will find, O Athenians! all ready to assist me, who have corrupted and injured their relatives, as Melitus and Anytus say. For those who have been themselves corrupted might perhaps have some reason for assisting me; but those who have not been corrupted, men now advanced in life, their relatives, what other reason can they have for assisting me, except that right and just one, that they know that Melitus speaks falsely, and that I speak the truth.

But why do some people like spending such a long time with me? You have heard why, Athenians! I have told you the whole truth, that they love hearing those who think they are wise but are not being closely questioned, for this is certainly not disagreeable. But I tell you that this duty was given to me by God, by oracles, by dreams, and by every other way in which God orders men to do things. All these things, Athenians, are true, and if they are not they are easy to prove false. For if I am now corrupting some of the young men, and have already corrupted others, surely some of them, having got older, will now have discovered that I gave them bad advice when they were young and would now rise up against me, accuse me and have me punished. Or if they didn't want to do this themselves, some of their family, their fathers, their brothers or other relatives, if their relation ever was damaged by me, would remember it. However, I can see that many of them are here: there is Crito, my contemporary and fellow townsman, father of Critobolus; there is Lysanius of Sphettus, father of Aeschines; there is Antiphon of Cephisus, father of Epigenes. There are those other people as well, whose brothers were just as close to me, namely, Nicostratus, son of Theodotus, brother of Theodotus—Theodotus is dead, so that he could not oppose what his brother is doing—and Paralus here, son of Demodocus, whose brother was Theages; and Adimantus, son of Ariston, whose brother is this Plato; and Æantodorus, whose brother is this Apollodorus. I could also mention many others, at least one of whom Melitus should have mentioned in his speech as a witness. However, if he forgot to do that, let him mention them now; I give him permission to do so, let him say it, if he has any allegation of that kind to make. But, it's rather contrary, you will find, Athenians. Everyone is ready to help me, even though Melitus and Antyus say that I have corrupted and harmed their relatives. Those who have been corrupted themselves might perhaps still help me; but those who have not been corrupted, their relatives, men now of advanced years, what other reason than they have for helping me, except the true and just one which is that they know Melitus is lying and that I am telling the truth?

23. Well, then, Athenians, these are pretty much the things I have to say in my defense, and others perhaps of the same kind. Perhaps, however, some among you will be indignant on recollecting his own case, if he, when engaged in a cause far less than this, implored and besought the judges with many tears, bringing forward his children in order that he might excite their utmost compassion, and many others of his relatives and friends, whereas I do none of these things, although I may appear to be incurring the extremity of danger. Perhaps, therefore, some one, taking notice of this, may become more determined against me, and, being enraged at this very conduct of mine, may give his vote under the influence of anger. If, then, any one of you is thus affected—I do not, however, suppose that there is—but if there should be, I think I may reasonably say to him: "I, too, O best of men, have relatives; for, to make use of that saying of Homer, I am not sprung from an oak, nor from a rock, but from men, so that I, too, O Athenians! have relatives, and three sons, one now grown up, and two boys: I shall not, however, bring any one of them forward and implore you to acquit me." Why, then, shall I not do this? Not from contumacy, O Athenians! nor disrespect toward you. Whether or not I am undaunted at the prospect of death is another question; but, out of regard to my own character, and yours, and that of the whole city, it does not appear to me to be honorable that I should do any thing of this kind at my age, and with the reputation I have, whether true or false. For it is commonly agreed that Socrates in some respects excels the generality of men. If, then, those among

you who appear to excel either in wisdom, or fortitude, or any other virtue whatsoever, should act in such a manner as I have often seen some when they have been brought to trial, it would be shameful, who appearing indeed to be something, have conducted themselves in a surprising manner, as thinking they should suffer something dreadful by dying, and as if they would be immortal if you did not put them to death. Such men appear to me to bring disgrace on the city, so that any stranger might suppose that such of the Athenians as excel in virtue, and whom they themselves choose in preference to themselves for magistracies and other honors, are in no respect superior to women. For these things, O Athenians! neither ought we to do who have attained to any height of reputation, nor, should we do them, ought you to suffer us; but you should make this manifest, that you will much rather condemn him who introduces these piteous dramas, and makes the city ridiculous, than him who quietly awaits your decision.

*Well then, Athenians, these are the things which I
have to say my defence, along with other things which
are similar. Perhaps, however, some of you might
object to my being so calm and not producing any
children or relatives and friends to beg the judges
with tears for mercy, as you may have done in cases
of far less importance; I do nothing like this, even
though I am in the most extreme danger. So perhaps
someone, noticing this, might become angry at my
conduct and vote against me. If anyone of you feels
like this–I don't suppose anyone does–but if anyone
does, I think I can fairly say to him, "Wonderful man,
I also have relatives, for to quote Homer, I did not
spring up from an oak or a rock but from men, so I
also, Athenians, have relatives, I have three sons, one
of them is now grown-up and two of them are boys:
however, I will not bring any one of them forward to
beg you to let me go." So why do I do not do this? It's
not from pride, Athenians, nor from disrespect
towards you. Whether or not I am scared of death is
another question, but to show respect for my own
character, and for yours, and for the whole city, I do
not think that at my age it would be honourable for
me to do anything like this, it would damage the
reputation I have, whether it is earned or not. For it
is generally agreed that in some ways Socrates is
better than other men. So those amongst you who
appear to be extremely wise, or strong, or to have any
other sort of virtue, were to behave in the fashion
which I have seen some do when they have been
brought to trial, it would be shameful, when they have
pretended to be one thing and then behaved in a
different fashion, as if dying would be if something*

dreadful for them to suffer, and as if they would be immortal if you did not execute them. Men like that seem to me to bring disgrace to the city, so that any foreigner might imagine that those Athenians who have most virtuous and who have been chosen above others to be magistrates and given other honours, are no better than women. Those of us who have gained any sort of reputation should not do these things, Athenians, and if we do, you should not tolerate it. You should make it plain that you would rather condemn anyone who tries these pathetic dramatics, and makes the city looked ridiculous, more than someone who quietly awaits his sentence.

24. But, reputation apart, O Athenians! it does not appear to me to be right to entreat a judge, or to escape by entreaty; but one ought to inform and persuade him. For a judge does not sit for the purpose of administering justice out of favor, but that he may judge rightly, and he is sworn not to show favor to whom he pleases, but that he will decide according to the laws. It is, therefore, right that neither should we accustom you, nor should you accustom yourselves, to violate your oaths; for in so doing neither of us would act righteously. Think not then, O Athenians! that I ought to adopt such a course toward you as I neither consider honorable, nor just, nor holy, as well, by Jupiter! on any other occasion, and now especially when I am accused of impiety by this Melitus. For clearly, if I should persuade you, and by my entreaties should put a constraint on you who are bound by an oath, I should teach you to think that there are no gods, and in reality, while making my defense, should accuse myself of not believing in the gods. This, however, is far from being the case; for I believe, O Athenians! as none of my accusers do, and I leave it to you and to the deity to judge concerning me in such way as will be best both for me and for you.

[Socrates here concludes his defense, and, the votes being taken, he is declared guilty by a majority of voices. He thereupon resumes his address.]

But apart from my reputation, Athenians, it doesn't seem right to me to beg a judge, or to escape through that begging. One should simply tell him the facts and try to persuade him. The judge is not here to give justice to those whom he favours, he is here to judge correctly, and he has sworn that he will not show favour just on his whims, but that he will decide according to the law. Therefore it is right that you should not become accustomed to violating your oaths, and we should not let you, because if we did both of us would be wrong. So do not think, Athenians, that I should behave towards you in a way which I would think would be dishonourable, unjust and impious, by Jupiter, on any other occasion, particularly now when this Melitus is accusing me of being impious. Clearly, if I manage to persuade you, and through my begging managed to turn those of you who are bound by an oath, I would be persuading you to think that there are no gods, and I would be acting as if I did not believe in the gods myself. However, this is far from the case; I do believe in the gods, Athenians, unlike my accusers, and I leave it to you and to God to judge in whatever way is best for me and for you.

[This here Socrates finishes his defence, and once the votes are counted he is declared guilty by a majority. He then carries on speaking.]

25. That I should not be grieved, O Athenians! at what has happened—namely, that you have condemned me—as well many other circumstances concur in bringing to pass; and, moreover this, that what has happened has not happened contrary to my expectation; but I much rather wonder at the number of votes on either side. For I did not expect that I should be condemned by so small a number, but by a large majority; but now, as it seems, if only three more votes had changed sides, I should have been acquitted. So far as Melitus is concerned, as it appears to me, I have been already acquitted; and not only have I been acquitted, but it is clear to every one that had not Anytus and Lycon come forward to accuse me, he would have been fined a thousand drachmas, for not having obtained a fifth part of the votes.

But I'm not upset, Athenians, that you have condemned me, along with everything else which has happened. I actually expected this to happen, in fact I'm rather surprised at the balance of the votes. I didn't expect to be condemned by such a small number, I thought there would be a great majority against me; however, it appears that if only three votes had changed sides, I would have been acquitted. I must say that it seems to me as far as Melitus is concerned, I have already been acquitted; not only have I been acquitted, but it's obvious to everyone that if Anytus and Lycon hadn't come forward to accuse me, he would have been fined a thousand drachma for not having been able to raise twenty percent of the vote.

26. The man, then, awards me the penalty of death. Well. But what shall I, on my part, O Athenians! award myself? Is it not clear that it will be such as I deserve? What, then, is that? Do I deserve to suffer, or to pay a fine? for that I have purposely during my life not remained quiet, but neglecting what most men seek after, money-making, domestic concerns, military command, popular oratory, and, moreover, all the magistracies, conspiracies, and cabals that are met with in the city, thinking that I was in reality too upright a man to be safe if I took part in such things, I therefore did not apply myself to those pursuits, by attending to which I should have been of no service either to you or to myself; but in order to confer the greatest benefit on each of you privately, as I affirm, I thereupon applied myself to that object, endeavoring to persuade every one of you not to take any care of his own affairs before he had taken care of himself in what way he may become the best and wisest, nor of the affairs of the city before he took care of the city itself; and that he should attend to other things in the same manner. What treatment, then, do I deserve, seeing I am such a man? Some reward, O Athenians! if, at least, I am to be estimated according to my real deserts; and, moreover, such a reward as would be suitable to me. What, then, is suitable to a poor man, a benefactor, and who has need of leisure in order to give you good advice? There is nothing so suitable, O Athenians! as that such a man should be maintained in the Prytaneum, and this much more than if one of you had been victorious at the Olympic games in a horserace, or in the two or four horsed chariot race: for such a one makes you appear to be happy, but I, to

be so; and he does not need support, but I do. If, therefore, I must award a sentence according to my just deserts, I award this, maintenance in the Prytaneum.

So, this man sentences me to death. Good. But what shall I give myself, Athenians? Isn't it clear that I will give myself what I deserve? So what is that? Do I deserve to suffer, or to pay a fine? Do I deserve this for deliberately not being quiet, but not going after what most men want, wealth, family matters, military commands, popular speechmaking, and all the jobs, conspiracies and factions that one meets the city, thinking that I was really too virtuous to be safe if I became involved in such matters? So I did not follow those pursuits, for by doing so I would have not been able to do any good for you or for me. However, in order to do each of you the greatest good privately, as I have said, I tried to do that, trying to persuade each one of you not to take care of any business before he had taken care of his own soul, and not taking care of the business of the city before he had taken care of the city itself, and to behave in this way in all things. So, seeing as that is what I have done, what treatment do I deserve? If I am judged by my true deserts, Athenians, I would deserve a reward, a reward appropriate to me. So then, what would be a suitable reward for a poor man, a do-gooder, the man who needs time in order to give you good advice? Nothing would be more appropriate than that a man like that should be kept in the city temple, he deserves it much more than somebody who has won a horse race at the Olympic Games, or the two or four horsed chariot race: someone like that makes you think you're happy, but I make you really happy; he does not need supporting, and I do. So if I were to give a sentence according to what I deserve, I would award myself a place in the city temple.

27. Perhaps, however, in speaking to you thus, I appear to you to speak in the same presumptuous manner as I did respecting commiseration and entreaties; but such is not the case, O Athenians! it is rather this: I am persuaded that I never designedly injured any man, though I can not persuade you of this, for we have conversed with each other but for a short time. For if there were the same law with you as with other men, that in capital cases the trial should list not only one day, but many, I think you would be persuaded; but it is not easy in a short time to do away with, great calumnies. Being persuaded, then, that I have injured no one, I am far from intending to injure myself, and of pronouncing against myself that I am deserving of punishment, and from awarding myself any thing of the kind. Through fear of what? lest I should suffer that which Melitus awards me, of which I say I know not whether it he good or evil? Instead of this, shall I choose what I well know to be evil, and award that? Shall I choose imprisonment? And why should I live in prison, a slave to the established magistracy, the Eleven? Shall I choose a fine, and to be imprisoned until I have paid it? But this is the same as that which I just now mentioned, for I have not money to pay it. Shall I, then, award myself exile? For perhaps you would consent to this award. I should indeed be very fond of life, O Athenians! if I were so devoid of reason as not to be able to reflect that you, who are my fellow-citizens, have been unable to endure my manner of life and discourses, but they have become so burdensome and odious to you that you now seek to be rid of them: others, however, will easily bear them. Far from it, O

Athenians! A fine life it would be for me at my age to go out wandering, and driven from city to city, and so to live. For I well know that, wherever I may go, the youth will listen to me when I speak, as they do here. And if I repulse them, they will themselves drive me out, persuading the elders; and if I do not repulse them, their fathers and kindred will banish me on their account.

However, perhaps by speaking to you like this you think that I'm speaking in the same arrogant fashion as I did when I was talking about begging judges, but this is not the case. The fact is that I am certain that I have never deliberately harmed any man, although I can't convince you of this, because we have only been speaking to each other for a little while. If the same law applied here as it does in other places, that in cases where execution is the punishment the trial should not just last a single day, but many days, I think you would agree with me, but it is not easy to refute great slanders in just a short time. So, certain that I have harmed nobody, I do not intend to harm myself, and to say that I deserve punishment and give myself anything like that. Through fear of what? In case I suffer through what Melitus gives me, which I have said I do not know if it is good or evil? Instead of this, would I choose what I certainly know is evil, and give myself that? Will I choose imprisonment? Why should I live in prison, as a slave for the established magistrates, the Eleven? Should I choose to be fined, and to be held in prison until it is paid? That'll be the same as what I mentioned before, because I do not have the money to pay. Shall I send myself into exile when? Perhaps you would agree to that. I would really be wanting to hang onto life, Athenians, if I were so foolish that I did not consider the fact that you, my fellow citizens, have found my way of life and speeches so tiresome and horrible that you want to get rid of them—how can I believe that others will put up with them. Far from it, Athenians! A fine life it would be for me at my age to have to wander around, thrown out of city after city, and live my life like that. For I know perfectly well that wherever I go, young men will listen to me when I speak, as they have done here. If they don't like what I say, they will throw me out themselves, persuading the elders to do so. If they do like what I say, their fathers and their families will banish me because of it.

28. Perhaps, however, some one will say, Can you not, Socrates, when you have gone from us, live a silent and quiet life? This is the most difficult thing of all to persuade some of you. For if I say that that would be to disobey the deity, and that, therefore, it is impossible for me to live quietly, you would not believe me, thinking I spoke ironically. If, on the other hand, I say that this is the greatest good to man, to discourse daily on virtue, and other things which you have heard me discussing, examining both myself and others, but that a life without investigation is not worth living for, still less would you believe me if I said this. Such, however, is the case, as I affirm, O Athenians! though it is not easy to persuade you. And at the same time I am not accustomed to think myself deserving of any ill. If, indeed, I were rich, I would amerce myself in such a sum as I should be able to pay; for then I should have suffered no harm, but now—for I can not, unless you are willing to amerce me in such a sum as I am able to pay. But perhaps I could pay you a mina of silver: in that sum, then, I amerce myself. But Plato here, O Athenians! and Crito Critobulus, and Apollodorus bid me amerce myself in thirty minæ, and they offer to be sureties. I amerce myself, then, to you in that sum; and they will be sufficient sureties for the money.

[The judges now proceeded to pass the sentence, and condemned Socrates to death; whereupon he continued:]

However, perhaps someone will say, Socrates, when you have left us, can you lead a silent and quiet life? This is the most difficult thing to persuade some of you of. I'm telling you that that would mean disobeying God, and so it is therefore impossible for me to live quietly, but if I say this you won't believe me, thinking I'm speaking ironically. On the other hand, if I say that the greatest good a man can do is to speak daily about virtue, and the other things you have heard me discussing, testing both myself and others, and that a life without questioning is not worth living, you would believe me even less. However, I swear to you, Athenians, that this is the case, although you are not easy to persuade. At the same time I don't think that I deserve any punishment. If I were rich, I would find myself a sum which I would be able to pay, for then I would have suffered no harm. However I cannot do that, unless you're willing to find me a sum which I can pay. Perhaps I could pay you a single silver coin: so I fine myself that. But here is Plato, and Crito Critobulus, and Apollodorus, encouraging me to fine myself thirty silver coins, and they offer to stand bail for me. So, I fine myself that amount; they guarantee the money.

[The judges now passed sentence, condemning Socrates to death; so he carried on:]

29. For the sake of no long space of time, O Athenians! you will incur the character and reproach at the hands of those who wish to defame the city, of having put that wise man, Socrates, to death. For those who wish to defame you will assert that I am wise, though I am not. If, then, you had waited for a short time, this would have happened of its own accord; for observe my age, that it is far advanced in life, and near death. But I say this not to you all, but to those only who have condemned me to die. And I say this, too, to the same persons. Perhaps you think, O Athenians! that I have been convicted through the want of arguments, by which I might have persuaded you, had I thought it right to do and say any thing, so that I might escape punishment. Far otherwise: I have been convicted through want indeed, yet not of arguments, but of audacity and impudence, and of the inclination to say such things to you as would have been most agreeable for you to hear, had I lamented and bewailed and done and said many other things unworthy of me, as I affirm, but such as you are accustomed to hear from others. But neither did I then think that I ought, for the sake of avoiding danger, to do any thing unworthy of a freeman, nor do I now repent of having so defended myself; but I should much rather choose to die, having so defended myself, than to live in that way. For neither in a trial nor in battle is it right that I or any one else should employ every possible means whereby he may avoid death; for in battle it is frequently evident that a man might escape death by laying down his arms, and throwing himself on the mercy of his pursuers. And there are many other devices in every danger, by

which to avoid death, if a man dares to do and say every thing. But this is not difficult, O Athenians! to escape death; but it is much more difficult to avoid depravity, for it runs swifter than death. And now I, being slow and aged, am overtaken by the slower of the two; but my accusers, being strong and active, have been overtaken by the swifter, wickedness. And now I depart, condemned by you to death; but they condemned by truth, as guilty of iniquity and injustice: and I abide my sentence, and so do they. These things, perhaps, ought so to be, and I think that they are for the best.

In order to save a rather short time, Athenians, you have let yourselves in for criticism from those who wish to attack the city, for having executed that wise man, Socrates. Those who want to criticise you will say that I'm wise, although I am not. If you had waited for a short time, this would have happened anyway; see how old I am, you can see that I am close to death. But I'm not saying this to all of you, only those who condemn me to death. And I say this, to the same people. Perhaps you think that I have been convicted because I did not have good enough arguments to persuade you, that if I had just said anything I could escape punishment. This is not the case: I have been convicted not because I did not have arguments, but because I do not have arrogance and impudence, and I will not just say things because you wanted to hear them, I will not lament and wail and do and say things which are unworthy of me, as you usually hear from others. I didn't think that I should, just to avoid danger, do anything unbefitting a freeman of Athens, and I do not regret having defended myself like this. I would much rather die than live having defended myself like that. It is not right in either a trial or battle for me or for anyone else to use any means possible to avoid death. In battle it is frequently obvious that a man could escape death by laying down his arms and surrendering to his enemies. In every dangerous situation there are techniques which would allow a man to avoid death, if he doesn't care what he does and says. Escaping death is not difficult, it is more difficult to avoid lowering oneself, that comes easier than death. And now I, being slow and old, have been caught by slow death, but my accusers, who are strong and active, have been caught by swift wickedness. And now I leave, condemned to death by you, but they are condemned by truth as being guilty of evil and injustice. I will wait for my sentence, and they will too. Perhaps things ought to be like this, and I think they are for the best.

30. In the next place, I desire to predict to you who have condemned me, what will be your fate; for I am now in that condition in which men most frequently prophesy—namely, when they are about to die. I say, then, to you, O Athenians! who have condemned me to death, that immediately after my death a punishment will overtake you, far more severe, by Jupiter! than that which you have inflicted on me. For you have done this, thinking you should be freed from the necessity of giving an account of your lives. The very contrary, however, as I affirm, will happen to you. Your accusers will be more numerous, whom I have now restrained, though you did not perceive it; and they will be more severe, inasmuch as they are younger, and you will be more indignant. For if you think that by putting men to death you will restrain any one from upbraiding you because you do not live well, you are much mistaken; for this method of escape is neither possible nor honorable; but that other is most honorable and most easy, not to put a check upon others, but for a man to take heed to himself how he may be most perfect. Having predicted thus much to those of you who have condemned me, I take my leave of you.

Next, I want to predict what fate has in store for those of you who have condemned me, for I am in the position in which men most frequently prophesy–that is, when they are about to die. So I say to you, Athenians, who have condemned me to death, that as soon as I am dead you will suffer a punishment far more severe, by Jupiter, than the one which you have given me. You have done this, thinking that it would free you from the obligation of having to account for your lives. However, I promise you that exactly the opposite will happen. There will be far more people accusing you, I have kept them back, although you did not know it; and they will be harder on you, because they are younger, and you will object more. If you think that by executing men you can stop people criticising you for not living well, you are very much mistaken. Escaping in this way is neither possible nor honourable; the most honourable and easiest thing to do is not to try and control others, but for each man to consider how he can make himself as perfect as possible. Now that I have predicted this for those of you who condemned me, I shall leave you.

31. But with you who have voted for my acquittal I would gladly hold converse on what has now taken place, while the magistrates are busy, and I am not yet carried to the place where I must die. Stay with me, then, so long, O Athenians! for nothing hinders our conversing with each other, while we are permitted to do so; for I wish to make known to you, as being my friends, the meaning of that which has just now befallen me. To me, then, O my judges! and in calling you judges I call you rightly—a strange thing has happened. For the wonted prophetic voice of my guardian deity on every former occasion, even in the most trifling affairs, opposed me if I was about to do any thing wrong; but now that has befallen me which ye yourselves behold, and which any one would think, and which is supposed to be the extremity of evil; yet neither when I departed from home in the morning did the warning of the god oppose me, nor when I came up here to the place of trial, nor in my address when I was about to say any thing; yet on other occasions it has frequently restrained me in the midst of speaking. But now it has never, throughout this proceeding, opposed me, either in what I did or said. What, then, do I suppose to be the cause of this? I will tell you: what has befallen me appears to be a blessing; and it is impossible that we think rightly who suppose that death is an evil. A great proof of this to me is the fact that it is impossible but that the accustomed signal should have opposed me, unless I had been about to meet with some good.

But I would gladly talk about what has happened with those of you who voted for my acquittal whilst the magistrates are busy, and I have not yet been taken off to the place of execution. So stay with me for this little time, Athenians, for there is nothing to stop us talking to each other while we can; I want to let you know, as my friends, the meaning of what has happened to me. A strange thing has happened to me, my judges (I'm giving you your correct name as my judges). The usual voice of prophecy which I have heard from my guardian deity in the past, even in the smallest matters, stopped me if I was about to do anything wrong. But now what you have seen has happened to me, which anyone would think is the worst that could possibly happen, the God did not give me any warning when I left home this morning, nor when I came to this court, nor as I was speaking; but on other occasions it has frequently stopped me in the middle of my speech. But now it never stopped me throughout this trial, in my actions or my words. Why do you think this is? I will tell you: what has happened to me is a blessing, and it is impossible for those who think correctly to imagine that death is an evil thing. I take it as a great proof that unless what is coming to me is good I would have received the usual signal to stop me.

32. Moreover, we may hence conclude that there is great hope that death is a blessing. For to die is one of two things: for either the dead may be annihilated, and have no sensation of any thing whatever; or, as it is said, there are a certain change and passage of the soul from one place to another. And if it is a privation of all sensation, as it were a sleep in which the sleeper has no dream, death would be a wonderful gain. For I think that if any one, having selected a night in which he slept so soundly as not to have had a dream, and having compared this night with all the other nights and days of his life, should be required, on consideration, to say how many days and nights he had passed better and more pleasantly than this night throughout his life, I think that not only a private person, but even the great king himself, would find them easy to number, in comparison with other days and nights. If, therefore, death is a thing of this kind, I say it is a gain; for thus all futurity appears to be nothing more than one night. But if, on the other hand, death is a removal from hence to another place, and what is said be true, that all the dead are there, what greater blessing can there be than this, my judges? For if, on arriving at Hades, released from these who pretend to be judges, one shall find those who are true judges, and who are said to judge there, Minos and Rhadamanthus, Æacus and Triptolemus, and such others of the demi-gods as were just during their own life, would this be a sad removal? At what price would you not estimate a conference with Orpheus and Musæus, Hesiod and Homer? I indeed should be willing to die often, if this be true. For to me the sojourn there would be admirable, when I

should meet with Palamedes, and Ajax, son of Telamon, and any other of the ancients who has died by an unjust sentence. The comparing my sufferings with theirs would, I think, be no unpleasing occupation. But the greatest pleasure would be to spend my time in questioning and examining the people there as I have done those here, and discovering who among them is wise, and who fancies himself to be so, but is not. At what price, my judges, would not any one estimate the opportunity of questioning him who led that mighty army against Troy, or Ulysses, or Sisyphus, or ten thousand others whom one might mention both men and women—with whom to converse and associate, and to question them, would be an inconceivable happiness? Surely for that the judges there do not condemn to death; for in other respects those who live there are more happy than those who are here, and are henceforth immortal, if, at least, what is said be true.

*Furthermore, we can conclude from this that there is
a great hope that death is a blessing. It can only mean
one of two things to die: either the dead are wiped
out, and cannot feel anything; or, as people believe,
the soul undergoes a change and moves from one
place to another. If it is the deprivation of all
sensations, as if it were a sleep in which you have no
dreams, death would be a wonderful thing. I think
that anyone, if he chose a night when he slept so
soundly that he did not dream, and compared it with
all the other nights and days in his life, and then was
asked to say how many days and nights had he spent
so pleasurably, I think that not only a private citizen
but even the great King himself would find that there
were only a small number. So, I say, if death is like
this, then it is a gain, for the whole of the future is
nothing more than a single night. But if, on the other
hand, death is moving from here to another place,
and what is believed is true, that all the dead who
have gone before are there, what greater blessing is
there, my judges? For if, in arriving in the
underworld, out of reach of those who pretend they
are judges, we find the true judges who are said to
judge there, Minos and Rhadamanthus, Aeacus and
Triptolemus, and other demigods who were just
during their lifetimes, would this be a cause for
regret? What would you give to have a meeting with
Orpheus and Musaeus, Hesiod and Homer? I would
be willing to die many deaths, if this is true. For me it
would be wonderful to travel there, where I could
meet with Palamedes, and Ajax, son of Telamon, and
any other of the ancients who died through an unfair
sentence. Comparing my sufferings with theirs would,*

I think, be rather wonderful. But my greatest pleasure would be to do what I have done on earth, to question and examine the people there and find out who is wise and who thinks he is but is not. What wouldn't you give, my judges, to have the chance of questioning the one who led that mighty army against Troy, or Ulysses, or Sisyphus, or ten thousand others whom one might mention, both men and women; can you imagine what happiness it would be to be able to meet them and speak to them and question them? I'm sure that the judges in the underworld will not sentence you to death for that; in some ways those who live down there are happier than those living on Earth, and once there they are immortal, if what is said is true.

33. You, therefore, O my judges! ought to entertain good hopes with respect to death, and to meditate on this one truth, that to a good man nothing is evil, neither while living nor when dead, nor are his concerns neglected by the gods. And what has befallen me is not the effect of chance; but this is clear to me, that now to die, and be freed from my cares is better for me On this account the warning in no way turned me aside; and I bear no resentment toward those who condemned me, or against my accusers, although they did not condemn and accuse me with this intention, but thinking to injure me: in this they deserve to be blamed.

Thus much, however, I beg of them. Punish my sons when they grow up, O judges! paining them as I have pained you, if they appear to you to care for riches or anything else before virtue; and if they think themselves to be something when they are nothing, reproach them as I have done you, for not attending to what they ought, and for conceiving themselves to be something when they are worth nothing. If ye do this, both I and my sons shall have met with just treatment at your hands.

But it is now time to depart—for me to die, for you to live. But which of us is going to a better state is unknown to every one but God.

So, my judges, you should look forward to death optimistically, and think about this one truth, that nothing is evil for a good man, neither while he is alive nor when he is dead, and the gods will not forget him. What has happened to me has not happened by chance; but it is clear to me, that it is better for me now to die and be released from my cares. This is why the warning did not come to turn me aside, and I have no resentment towards those who condemned me, or those who accused me, although they did not condemn and accuse me meaning for this to happen, but thinking that they were injuring me: they deserve to be criticised for that.

However, I beg this favour from them. When my sons grow up, punish them, give them the same pain I have given you, if they seem to care about riches or anything else before goodness; if they think that they are something when they are nothing, criticise them as I have criticised you, for not paying attention to what they should, and for thinking that they are something when they are worth nothing. If you do this for me, my sons and I will both have had good treatment from you.

But now it is time to go–I am going to die, you're going to live. But only God knows which of us is going to a better place.

Made in the USA
Las Vegas, NV
09 October 2024